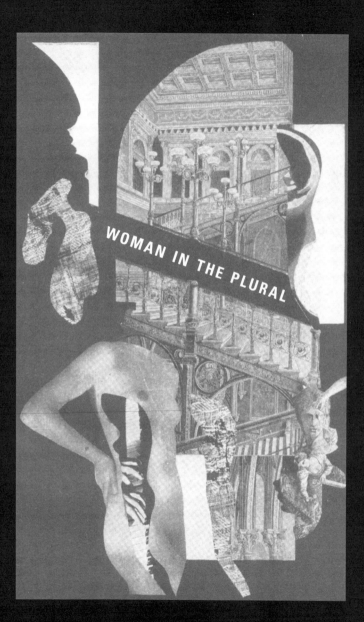

WOMAN IN THE PLURAL

Vítězslav Nezval

WOMAN IN THE PLURAL

Translated from the Czech
by Stephan Delbos & Tereza Novická

TWISTED SPOON PRESS

PRAGUE

2021

ISBN 978-80-86264-56-1 (hardcover)
ISBN 978-80-86264-98-1 (e-book)

This translation was made possible by a grant
from the Ministry of Culture of the Czech Republic.

MINISTERSTVO
KULTURY

CONTENTS

1

WOMAN IN THE PLURAL

The windmill of their arms waves me a greeting
The coffee grinder or street organ of endless chatter lulls me to sleep
They are nothing and everything like a prophecy
                                        from tablecloth creases
The body of the dearest is from over-starched canvas
They stroll and stroll through the horsetail of flunkeys
Perfumed with the very midnight of beech solitudes
Down bearhide streets doused with evening's swill
Their gaze blurred rain or the coolness of cupboards
                                        moves me to tears
They stroll decomposing and composing themselves in my dream
                        which is a card index of heart spade and club aces
At every intersection their cries like black mullein terrify
                                        the eyes of machines
They stop traffic these ridiculous tearoom puppets
And light the fuses of aching anarchists
One is petite all question mark and rooster comb she treads softly
                                        whip in hand
As if commanding red pantaloons in riding school
She hounds a chess-playing flea
A veritable miracle of willow wicker woven with bast
Another a darker spool of twine threaded with black beads
Asserts her will with a high-heel of well-hidden dynamite
A telegraphist of always encrypted messages
Losing on each stair a carnation honeycomb or brush
I adore her throat of lavender soap
She fans in the stable of random passageways

Her sandalwood hand plucks the bouquet of her own neck
of foamy dandelion
To erase the last searing spark of day
Her breasts purr like a cat
In the cold as a marble staircase cascade gushes at her
She feels them now only in a stomach pure as a white
camphor compress
Or under eyelids concealing the icy wafer of her chocolate gaze
A third is a fiery redhead like a nest of salamanders
With thighs of semolina coarsened by a kiss
She lifts her arm to whack a crested lark
Fastened by two sapphire studs her head is a case for my
two precious medallions
A storeroom of old relics I must fight through to reach her now
transformed into an armchair
Neither naked nor clad in fishnet nor affirming life in any other way
Eternally craving like the slumber of ruminants and convulsive
like the spring of a divan
Devoted to the variable fall of checkers dice and dominoes
like the shuttle of a sewing machine
Never again will I encounter a woman of bath sponge
With sweat trickling from her nettle wig she doesn't wait
to be addressed
On a moonlit night her shadow sinks slowly into the slaked
lime of a brickyard
Her lips can be chewed like jelly
Tall lamps or rusted oakum
On sweltering days along high riverbanks girls wash flyspecked
summer off their shoulders

Young pear-shaped mothers and the midnight swooning
                              of widowed scallops
My desire to carry them from the burning building singes me
                         like the straw of their tresses

SONG OF SONGS

Your eyes two gunshots fired blindly
Two gunshots fired blindly right on target
Two gunshots fired blindly around the corner I turned
Like a convict looking for the prison yard's end
Your eyes two party horns
Two distant carousels
Two bells
Two signets
Your eyes two thimbles of hemlock
Your eyes two gags for eternal silence
Two wicker baskets
Two test tubes
Two brass clock wheels
Your eyes two buttercups
Your eyes two perfect rhymes
Your eyes two field drums
Two sad funerals two window leaps
Your eyes two dreamless nights
Like apothecary scales
Like a double-barreled shotgun
Like a dual adieu
Your eyes like two cactus flowers
Like a single dumbbell
Like a two-volume novel
Like a ripped rose
Like the Tropic of Cancer with the Tropic of Capricorn
Like a fake ducat beside a real ducat

Like two disc brakes
Like sea and land like the Gemini like two timid sighs
Your lips are a red order
One salutes and stands at attention
As you withdraw you're attended by eyes right
Of all those who swore an oath to you
Your lips are a soft velvet ribbon
Happily leaning over the tobacco plant
An eruption from the crater of a rose
A blowfly of sunstrokes
Your lips two spawning fish
A tinderbox with touchwood
A spice grinder
Your lips two award ribbons
Your lips are red-hot coals I stoke to burn my memories
And a huge carnivorous plant
A cockscomb
A breakfast plum cake
Your lips are a bleeding truffle
And a summer beehive
Your lips are an enigmatic monogram
Your lips are a weaving shuttle painted red
Your lips are a sugar bowl
But also a field of red poppies full of statues
Your lips are a golden spinning wheel
A seabed a moon crater
Your lips are a case for pearls
A sealed last will
A blazing skyrocket
A watch spring

Your lips are a lunar eclipse
A solar eclipse
An eclipse of Venus and Earth
Your hands are scissors that cut through my dream
Your hands spiders
As your shoulders quiver like a peacock
Your hands are ice packs
Your hands are flower buds
Your hands are raindrops
On breasts forming a vortex
Your breasts are phantasms
Like puffball dust clouds
Your breasts are like a cyclone concealing two ruby flames
Your breasts are a wasp's nest
An hourglass two piles of semolina
A frozen bird
Your breasts are two oil lamps
Two hogtied hostages
Neon arrows
Boiling cream
Your breasts are snakes basking in the sun
Two corks in water
Two solitary mushrooms
Your breasts erect as a porcupine
Your breasts taking flight
Your breasts are two camellias in the hands of night
Two pigeons in a thief's clutches
Two dandelions
Your breasts like a jingle bell duet
Like opal

Like two whip cracks
Like baby cauliflower
Like two knots in a kerchief
Like the rising and setting sun like rising and setting Venus and Jupiter
Your belly is a fireball
With the scent of singed hair
Your belly is a rattan ladder
A storm at sea and the saddest reef
Your belly is a fowl with a turkey's wattle
A colossal leech
A skid on black ice
Your belly is aquatic nettle
Horseradish leaf or a lapping flame
Your belly is a mill
And also the mill wheel pulverizing a drowned corpse
A breaking wheel
A white louse with mandibles clasped in prayer
Your belly is whitewash
Kneaded dough a white-hot fork
A kangaroo overwintering
A dim mirror and undersea evening
Your belly a cloud before a storm
A pond amid a moonlit night
Your belly of organdy soaked in black ink
Your sex is a marvelous deception
Will-o'-the-wisp or sage
Your sex is a split willow whistle
Like the residue of reseda soap
Like the mouth of an earthworm
Like a baby peapod

Like a moist affectionate eye
Like a *Libellula*
Like a *Mimosa*
Your sex like a firefly in the heart of a cabbage rose
As if you're from black elderberry marrow
From white asbestos fiber glowing in the fire
From a mix of magnolia dough and dark rye flour
From worm-eaten rose mahogany
Your legs are the clash of two flashes of sheet lightning
Of two melancholies
Of two lengthy rivers
Your legs like water beetles
Like magnesium flashes
Like winter nights
Like long equations
Your legs like drunken grape harvests
Like a harbor dance
Your legs like war
Your crotch is a soldering flame
A butterfly's flight a ship's propellor
Your hips are a cavalcade
Your hips are Geissler tubes
Your hips are indolence itself
A spindle's hum a viola's shadow
Your brow is a spark
Your teeth a press
Your ears stray question marks
Your neck a waterfall
You are like day fading into night fading into day fading
                                        into phantasm

A CHEMISE

Strange nameless beings enthrall me
Their history plain as Gibraltar
They are the bastards of reality and wind that wandered Africa
The Angelus chimes

One of those sweltering nights at the end of June 1935
I walked past the Luxembourg Gardens
The clock was striking twelve
And the streets were empty
As delivery vans and desolate as Ash Wednesday
I thought of nothing
And desired nothing
I desired nothing was in no hurry nothing weighing on me
I walked like a man without memory
A shell of a person
I walked like an old man who no longer needs sleep

I don't know what suddenly captured my attention I recall my sigh
The trees in the Luxembourg Gardens were full of white gauze
I gazed at those paper bandages
Through the iron fence
And maybe I was even singing

That is all
And Paris sold into slavery
Writhed in a frenzy

O Paris shackled by your bridges
Prague Paris Leningrad and all the other cities I have wandered
I see that herd of fettered women
Drowned still ablaze under open sky
Just like their manacles trampled by crowds
O archway of bridges
I see a single city
Through which flow the Seine Neva and Vltava
And a brook where countrywomen do the laundry
The brook I live beside

Windows
Through one a statue from Place du Panthéon enters my room
A second faces Charles Bridge
From a third I look onto Nevsky Prospekt
But there are even more windows

I always loved the paper cones of street vendors
Whose secrets I have yet to discover
They remind me of an empty laundry room
And a pile of chemises
A chute the common grave of nameless women
I know of a forest where wide burdock leaves conceal a girl's bosom
A tin cross with her white arms
A sofa whose stuffing reeks of disinfectant

Who are you I always see as a sewing machine
This evening I speak of Boulevard du Montparnasse resembled you
I was sitting in front of Café du Dôme

Looking at the ornamentation on a building's sixth floor
It felt like it was snowing
In my mind I was celebrating the last New Year's Eve
                                                    of the nineteenth century
A landau parked beneath a tree full of song
I tried in vain to find the house with the sewing machine
                                from whose shuttle I would have liked a thread
Then I walked toward the Luxembourg Gardens

It is beautiful how the gardeners protect the fruit on trees
                                                    with little pouches
Like you cover your naked breasts in a chemise
Beautiful as a pail of water tipped over in a funeral home
Beautiful as a needle in birch bark with a carved date
Beautiful as a poppyhead touched by a bell
Beautiful as a slipper floating in floodwaters by a window
                                                    with an oil lamp
Beautiful as a woodpile where a butterfly sits
Beautiful as a roasted apple in snow
Beautiful as a bed frame struck by a fireball
Beautiful as a wet rag in flames
Beautiful as a loaf of bread on the sidewalk at midnight
Beautiful as a button on a monastery wall
Beautiful as a treasure in a flowerpot
Beautiful as a spiritist's table scribbling on a gate
Beautiful as a wreath in a shooting range
Beautiful as scissors snipping a candlewick
Beautiful as a tear in the eye
Beautiful as the capillary tissue of a watch in a horse's ear

Beautiful as a diamond in a condottiere's musket
Beautiful as tooth prints in an apple
Beautiful as the trees in the Luxembourg Gardens wrapped
in starchy linen

METEOR

I know a district where man is wind and woman a lamp
Windows here form a game of dominoes
A district of salt pillars
Cesareaned from other streets
A double-decker leper ship
You would think it were a large hairdressers' enterprise
Elegant bosoms
A textile mill of hairdos
A cemetery where allegories kneeling in windows keep vigil
                                     over a guttering candle
A cemetery of cats' eyes
With an auditorium inside
An auditorium with the attributes of a waxworks and
                                        a dissecting room
Hatless men give mouth-to-mouth
To drowned women lying in stalls
Women birds are also present
They throw themselves at the bodies of young men brought in
                                 through the window by flood
An eternal flame sheds tears above the sink
A violin coming alive inside a cabinet
An outfit on a hanger as if somebody were hanged
A star peeks through a crack in the ceiling
Or a mouse
To this day I wander these wooden stairs in my dreams
Where are you
O women morphed into a meteor

What a bouquet you would make for the world's saddest town square
I see your geyser dying out
You are like a scourge for flogging the fantasies
Merging in my memory
Flare up once more like a rosary of lightbulbs

                          with burned-out filaments

I toss the grenade that hit me

Again I unfasten the bodice to embrace you skeleton

                              covered in cobwebs

Hello rubber tub
A gypsy woman lolling like a cloud
The reseda of their tuberculosis will never fade from my memory
Only to me was she a guelder rose
For you I will love Indian clubs
That night I buried my love in a crumbling stove
She sang like coiled cord
She mimics an overturned kettledrum the morning of a

                              great celebration

The rainbow of a sentimental afternoon
I follow a sack of flour down the stairs
A miraculous mealworm suddenly lying there
Farewell disrobing rose
And all at once it disintegrated before my eyes
Her singing lips are a raspberry wellhead
Strange as a muff box
Across a huge belly I spotted laughter with fly eyes
Beautiful as an ear of corn
She passed an all-night pharmacy like murder from mouth to mouth
This time I entered to a nun nailed to the wall

Ten or fifteen strawflowers I mistook for sunflowers
And a whole herd of creatures made from soap of multiple odors
I don't have the strength to dig in every box of their wigs
Wigs with the hue of all lethargic evenings
O meteors

A toxic celebration with no end in sight
My nights like flames on flagpoles
Like tinted forests
Like gardens of menthol
Like harbor chanties
Like skies upholstered in shrimp
Like long rollers brimming with ants
Like cookie cutters
Like cork storms
Like a museum of *Carabus*
Like alchemists' athanors
My nights like the meeting of flies and lanterns over a pile of feathers
Like the meeting of towers and naked women
Like the meeting of trumpets with bird nests
Like the meeting of terraces and loud thunderclaps
Like the meeting of spades with spring water
Like the meeting of apothecary scales with a flash of ruby
My nights like headless poppies
Recede along torn-up train tracks
Behind circus wagons where blind men in whiteface soundly
                                                    sleep my days

Blinded by the meteor

WOMEN FROM THE OUTSKIRTS

Every night they place the poverty of their fingers under seal
And head out hatted
With the ruby of summer and papilionaceous flowers
From houses with consumptive blotches

The thrushes know them
And seeking the night
Scatter from a closed window
Awaiting new tenants

A cat three moths and the moon
But no light inside
Only the slippers of errant occupants
Hesitant like their wearers

The town is visible just beyond the walls
Bells answer one another while people dine in silence
You would think a fire had erupted below
And panic grips the women from the outskirts

Their eyes are used to piercing the darkness like cats' eyes
And they will hypnotize me
When I return home so that I won't want to turn on the lights
When I'm dreaming so that I won't want to wake before dusk

Their mouths are used to staying silent
And chewing their cabbage rose
I wish I could pick up from the street
Where a black hearse has passed

Their legs are used to propelling sewing machines
And moving like a cradle
How I would love to surrender to their heady lullaby
My sleepless nights my convulsive fevers

Their breasts dispel darkness
Like theater floodlights
I would follow to where
We fall through the trapdoor

Their auburn curls
Have the scent of cellars
I loved to enter like a monk
With a forbidden hymnal

Their fingers are used to the thimble
Like those of other women are to gold
Which I hate like altars and military medals
Like dentures like fireproof safes

Their fingers never make the sign of the cross
On the foreheads of the great cousins
When they depart for the square with the red banners
Of that volcano whose furnace will soon go out

Their fingers are jabbed by needles
Like those of other women are jabbed by kisses
Of chivalry that has replaced love
Poetry and everything I've ever held dear

And for which I wander to the outskirts
For nothing more than a dream
Of those great young ladies from the outskirts
Whose evenings uncork the champagne of freedom

O rave O rave
Until I imagine I hear
The beat of a tarantella
Beneath the Bastille of our evenings bathed in red sky

1.

She was squatting over Carthusian pinks astride a balk
As if flung from the shoulder of a horrible man
A horrible chimney sweep
His blackened hand
Left no trace anywhere else
Not even on the door or knob
A chimney sweep who likely pays women
That day I was terrified

2.

She stood on a stepladder in the chapel dusting the starry heavens

with a rag

On a stepladder where a brush lay
When she climbed down
The brush was gone
I searched for it in every room

3.

Kneeling on a branch she plucked ripe apples
I gazed at the wasp's nest
Caught on her skirt and buzzing like a blowfly
That day I killed a thousand flies

4.

Bent over blackberry bushes
She left a thorn embedded in her body
A rose thorn
I searched for her on every balk

5.

The chimney sweep returned
Oh how I laughed at him
I smashed the wasp's nest with the brush
And pared off every thorn in the garden

SHADOW OF A CORSET

Tell me reed bouquet
Which city's entrails have I come through
Its battering ram pounds
While someone unlaces you

A tower of plates
Pressed me to its base
I know nothing

My blindness and I
From the diver's trade we've retained without recollection
                            only the pleasure of holding our breath
Nostalgia for the elastic city
And a passion for seeking its ruins

A magnificent accordion leaves me breathless
The ocean's breast swells unfurling from the deep
The shutter goblin moves its lips and whistles
Somewhere a tire deflates

Still the corset like a paneless window
Lies on the table as snow falls
From its cracked cask
I catch just a whiff of the grape harvest

DUEL

She shoos the fowl of her fingers
Into the midst of whiskers of a man straining like barley
While her back cascades like rain
Down the bidet of her buttocks

This unfair fight
Old codger with statue
Ends in three slashes of a dagger
Yet the murderer

Collapsing before his victim
Sees with shut eyes red poppies
Scorching his beard like a flame
Of gratification never attained

WOMEN AFTER BATHING

The thrushes of their tanned shoulders drive summer
                                 out of every mouse hole
They lie like soaked bed sheets
And their fingers read the alphabet of the blind in the grass

The choral chant of their tree frogs
Keeps me from sleep
So I lift my head to the shutter of their embrace
With a hint of the evening star

A whole regiment of lissome women
Maneuvers with paper cones
Whose secrets will be revealed by broad-chested female pugilists

Buttoned-up summer
Unbuttons to let her breasts swing free
No Angelus ever rang louder
Than these two bells shuddering all the bamboo rafters

PHANTOMS

Larvae of a smile split like a pillory
Larvae of a sorrow looking for funereal nail polish
They walk past us leering
Vacant bodies resembling fencers' jackets

They flaunt lightning that does not sear
They flaunt a star of breasts bursting open like a hardened boil
Their egg-shaped faces the color of Easter are there as a pedestal
For the most lavish hats

O women I pursue your phantom
Ever illusory
As I once pursued a dragonfly
As I pursue a geese procession of clouds unstuck from the sky

What are you but spectrally floating bras
Torsos of rubber legs billowy shirts a ditty invites to dance
What are you but huge ideal bagpipes
Played by our sex-starved sleep

I kiss the reseda of your fingertips
Only for my love of giddiness
Without ever trusting a shred of your false promises
I kiss them like a handkerchief is kissed

You are like porcelain dolls rattling inside
Above all else I love that poppyhead noise
Your eyes shed opiates
Your eyes smoldering like a snuffed wick

I admire you at the spa
When you parade the neon violins of your bodies
Awaiting a musician
To free the willow of their fairy tale

You cuddle the gaze of men in the crook of your arm
Like an invisible newborn
You would love to serve as I would you Enchantress
When my gaze follows the caravan of your swaying hips

Your gaze is the roar from the blue of a beehive
That is you and your queen
Who has hidden and for whom you die
Murdered by your own sting

You are most captivating on the promenade
In enormous chinchilla furs
That make of you werewolves
Whose artistry you are happy to flaunt

Outcome uncertain like a game of cards
Shuffled by the wind suffused with perfumes
Whether you are a seven or an ace
That selfsame back always titillates me

Sometimes the phantom vanishes and a woman emerges
I know this moment well precious as a future
When you all will discard your chrysalis disguise
And simplicity will be given its due

Our poems shall be cursed
Like bacteria so sublime under a microscope
That blooms best in the enervated blood
Of our debilitated century

A century of calamity and poetry
We've come to consummate
That will decline in a more bearable age
Like a high fever

But this morning or tomorrow evening
I will encounter a new procession of women
Even more spectral
Than cylinders full of rarefied hydrogen

They will be real girls bats
And the most fascinating perversions
The likes of which even hashish eaters have never dreamed
Will be born in their beds

Their eyes will be of atropine
Their arms linked in a carousel
Passion will quarter them
And drag them before us on horses' tails

Those marvelous blondes more sultry than a hothouse
Those brunettes like Saharan nights
For whom my imagination burns like malaria
Its lazaretto filled with specters

Where Woman appears in countless variations
Woman who will never disappoint me
Woman in the plural
Woman who will never mourn me

A PROPHECY

One summer night I will walk through a city foreign to me
A city where I know no one
A city where a celebration just ended
It will feel like a Sunday
I will walk past an immense structure
A bizarre building
Perhaps a museum of stuffed birds
The hour when the sun sets
The streets will be deserted
Suddenly I will stop
As a woman appears at the corner of the building
Woman fountain
Slender
And slightly overdressed for summer
In fox fur
And her hat will conceal half her face
She will be somewhat taken aback
She will think she knows me I will think I know her
She will look around
And only then answer my greeting
I will tell her everything
About the strange premonition haunting me for years
Whenever I walk past a certain building in a city I do not love
This city will always remain foreign to me
Though I am not here for the first time
My premonition clings to me
The premonition that I will meet her here

The woman will smile once I finish explaining
She will not ask me anything
Nor will we tell our names
We will walk together turning left
Passing through a rather large park
I do not know who will lead whom when we take a route
I've never taken

We will enter a building she has the key to
We will cross the courtyard
And then climb a very dilapidated stairway to the fourth floor
She will say she has lived alone
Since the day her parents died
The room we enter will be old fashioned
Not a single thing changed she will say since she's almost always gone
And only returns to the apartment for short spells
She will light a table lamp
Ask me to take a seat
Sitting herself on a vintage divan
Not even removing her hat
She will tell me she adores fantastical stories
And old German Romanticism

Come at last
Most real woman and most real phantom
You for whom all my poems have been written
So I may kneel before your eyes
Woven by summer night a merciless spinner
So I may blush before the mirror of your brow
As soon as you reveal yourself to me starfish or stalagmite
Your feet soaking in the world's darkest bath fascinate me

Now today when I pass through the murk of passageways
The vitality of your hands is stored in the coldest cellar of terror
Your lips are the bloodiest of all murders
You have traveled half the world like a sleepwalker
Only to wake from your dreams in different beds
Callous as rain fickle as a damselfly
Come for the allure of a single evening
I am absolutely certain I'll never see you again once your door
                                        clicks shut behind me
When night passes like a fireball
Never again will I be able to sleep in that city you keep returning to
Like an exhausted comet

Again summer
I peer at certain hazy evenings
When a celebration seems to have ended
I fix my eyes on the walls of that imaginary museum
Where the fires have gone out
I look at the features of a deserted street
As if before a curtain
That conceals the future
I am happy
Because her footsteps draw near
Though circuitously
Down the boulevards of the most distant cities
Her steps draw near I can already hear them
They startle the pigeons of countless Venices
To me the sun sets just for her
And she will appear right on time
No way for me to miss her

I can already smell her scent
O coffined streets
I sense her approaching like we sense the approach of our death

SHOPWINDOWS

When I feel I am most faithful to you
When I avert my eyes from other women
Beware
It is not a ruse
Nor is it the truth
It is self-deceit
For a long time I didn't understand what shopwindows meant to me
For a long time I didn't understand their allure
And yet I have them to thank for the magic of my walks
Little stationery shops particularly move me
I buy green ink
Unconscious that I'm pursuing a green-eyed woman
Silken stationery
Like their lingerie
I need none of it
Just as I have no need for a leather cigar case
That enamors me
Like a mulatto's vulva
O women the shape of tobacco pipes
Slim robust the gently curving back
Women with the mechanism of the most delicate instruments
With the chattering tongue of a watch
With breasts of magnifying glasses
Poised like pince-nez
With eyes giving the opaque impression of moonstones
With the tongue of a baby bottle
With hips of transparent glass retorts

With hands of communicating vessels
With the embrace of a magnet
I also pause in front of delicatessens
Where their nipples make currant jam captivating
And where they hide their breasts in jars of peeled peaches
Their gazes are black cherries
Peering demonically
With the sex of young girls under artichoke leaves concealed

        by a hand

With the repulsive sex of date fruit
Of pickled mushrooms
With the sex of a sliced melon
With the tongue of a mirabelle plum
It is evening
Naked they peep out from under muslin drapes
Offering an eager hand their glove
They smile from the darkness of mirrors
I walk for hours
Aroused beyond words
And even at night I see them emerging from a pool of floral

        still lifes

Their desire resembles orchids
As my desire resembles gladiolas
My desire like a pliable watch spring
Like the cap of an inkwell popping open
Like the locomotion of a caterpillar in a rose
Like the cocking of a rifle's hammer
Like the rotations of a coffee grinder
Like the quivering eye of a neon sign
Like a barometer

My desire for which I have no name
My desire for notebooks never to be written in
My desire for books I will never read
My desire that awakens without reason and disappears
Like a needle in the hands of a skilled seamstress
My desire for all women
Enchanted like a ballgown in a hazelnut
Like a star in fire
Like a stream in wood
Like joy in tears
Like life in death
My desire that makes me a sleepwalker
O moons of my walks

When I feel I am most faithful to you
I deceive you most
You deceive me most
You who would like to buy up the world
You most delicate you most faithful
You who are a woman and a child
A woman and anything from reality
A woman and anything
A woman and the sum of all shopwindows and wonders of nature

TO A LITTLE GIRL

You are like a toy box
Two balls tumbled from
You press them in your hands
And glare defiantly
Like your bony knees
Grimacing at the entire world
You are like a box for a meerschaum cigar holder

MAIDENHOOD

Their maidenhood is a thimble
I search for
With bee-stung finger

LITANY

Woman passing by you
Ray of a needle and thunderous orchestras you
Gum tree you
Honeycomb nailed to the ceiling of evening you
Haunted house shaped like a glove you
Tip of a match and scales you
Moonlit watering hole you
Pyre of wigs and jasmine blossoms you
Kiss of a wellspring and flight of a wild goose you
Diamonds strewn on glaze ice you
Child's smile above an astronomical chart you
String emitting a flageolet tone you
Tree made of sheep's wool you
Sailboat propelled by a cigar puff you
Starry night salvo you
Cone of rose petals and Batavian tears you
Moon in a cat's eye you
Upanishad of Upanishads you
Lightning-scorched bush of lace you
Organdy mask you
Music of zither and samovar you
Gale girded by a wisp of straw you
Haven of fogs and hibernating birds you
Lamp flashing signals to honor Tristan's arrival you
Bank of snowflakes you
Torch of hair on sunflower heads you
Marble bridge over silent tears you

Rainbow comprising a periscope you
Dormant flute the shape of scissors you
Hunting song and glade a doe visits at night you
Ball of butterflies and needles you
Echoes of a dream and a cuckoo you
Tower of May rain you
Praying mantis devouring the sleep of men you
Bee hibernating on the lips of a candelabrum you
Glitter of a salt room and mirrors you
Spiny dye-murex I play songs on like on a comb
O woman of flame
Woman who returns to me in cards
Woman of my tantalizing tortures
Woman with spinning-wheel eyes
Woman with a mother-of-pearl windmill
Woman merciless as malaria
Woman with a dress train of swollen streams
Woman with bony fingers that will press my eyes shut one last time

NATURE

I finally tossed my old biology textbook into the fire
What good could Linnaean taxonomy still do me
I am a human being that means I am sentient
And I want to communicate with people about all the mysteries
Let others investigate the nature of matter
I investigate the nature of my emotions
And I give things new names
To define their human equation
I was born during the first days of the twentieth century
My childhood played with different marvels than children of the
                                        nineteenth century did
Machines too played a part in my games
I was an unwitting witness to the blossoming of all sciences
Before my eyes strolled women formed by fashion
All of humanity in those days took on a strange wholly novel flavor
Behold the dictionary of my senses
This time I want to express most precisely what nature means to me
My poetry is not the poetry of falling leaves
And I never pick flowers on my walks
I mix up their names
For I walk past them too excited by my own subjectivity
Here it is a simple valley
A thistle swab pregnant with sweet narcotic makes me tremble
Its stem coarse as mountain hamlets
The land splitting open gives way to iodoform goslings
Bumblebees buzz like spluttering wicks
The willow a winnower

A hedgehog ball of yarn that knits its own socks
A weaving shuttle scuttles through the grass
Greetings summer Saturday
Your geese are honking ocarinas
Bleach caked in lime
Pouches of feathers
Boisterous howitzers
Your songbirds are the barbs on an invisible fence
Splinters stuck in the throat
Sparks off sugarloaves sprinkled with poppy seed
The murmur of electrical discharge
The audio signal of towers
Flutes of the stars
Your cornflower is a virgin's sigh
A pearl's voice a child's tears
Your lindens are crammed drugstores
An ironing shop for bonnets
A noisy bazaar
The forests of your nettles are nothing but short circuits
Pincushions
Your rabbit is a lost muff
Your deer carry inundated chairs through the woods
Your forests walk around in bowler hats
Your broom shrub is a child licking her fingers
Your leafy knoll is a discarded Inverness cape
Your field balks are the rags of a tramp with a cravat
                              the gaudy color of crown vetch
Your lawn is a dubious storehouse of small round boxes
Your dandelions are your laundry day
And your lime quarries your dank washhouse

Your gardens are a theater's storeroom of assorted costumes
Your gardens are pianos
Your gardens are feature films
Ceremonious parliaments chess tournament venues
Autumn is here again
With vineyards that swell like rheumatics
With the toothless mouths of showers
With the buckshot of downpours
With the briquettes of plowed fields
With the embroidered towel of meadow saffron
With the coathangers of bare branches
With the soap of field paths
With cockades of rose hip
With crows that resemble cracked clogs
With the twine of the last weeds
With the stale slabs of moss-covered walls
With the sleigh bells of plums
With the wet rag of cabbage stumps
With the tailor's iron of molehills
With the pennywhistles of dusks
With the rolled-up sleeves of icy mornings
With the cobbler's glue of overripe medlars
With the lolling tongues of night frosts
With the anthills of incessant mists
But I still have a greater dread of winter
Its clay like a toothless currycomb
Its accordions of well-trodden furrows
Its scalped trees
Its eggs lining the length of the valley
Its crate entered barefoot by its rain showers

By its rivers and streams
By its gullies
Its snowflakes merciless as a candle snuffer
Its blizzards of volcanic yeast
Its double wardrobe of eternal icebergs
Its dusty mill of evenings
Its goosebumps of mange between its toes of shrubs
Its bearded heads sticking out of the chimney
Its scrub brush of snowstorms on the stairway of night
O spring
The blades of your rivers rotate again
You blow a tune on a comb of fence pickets
Your birds like keyholes peep into every trunk of the valley
Your first skylark is a drop of raspberry on a tongue of fire
On a tongue coated in white film on a feverish tongue
Your first snowdrop is a child's thumb on a white quilt
Your first primrose is the full freshness of girls' saliva
The full freshness of the tips of their breasts
The full freshness of their lips
The full freshness of their raspberry-scented wombs

2

PAGES FROM A DIARY

During the night of May 5–6, 1935, I had an unpleasant dream about Miss K. I didn't write it down in time, so my memory has retained only these details: In the dream K. had come to Prague. I apparently met her in company. I spoke to her as if nothing had ever happened between us. She took offense, replying: "Is that all?" I accompanied her to the Hotel Neptune. On the stairs we met an older woman I recognized as a spy. She evidently was there to catch us in flagrante. I also suspected that she was in cahoots with K. Were they colluding? The dream faded.

•

On May 6, the thought of K. spontaneously came to mind during the day. Because I had just gotten my fountain pen back from the repair shop, it seemed to me an especially opportune moment to write her a letter, purely informative, addressing several of her rather urgent questions. I did not write the letter.

•

The unpleasant aspect of the dream most likely originated in the recent comments of a friend, who repeated as faithfully as possible the vile calumnies two of my enemies were spreading about K.

•

On the afternoon of May 6, for no reason, I put on a suit I rarely wear, that I had last worn when I went out with K. Everything urged me to spend the day not working. I took a walk across Pohořelec and down Úvoz Street past those charming house signs that I love so much, all the way to Charles Bridge. Jindřich Honzl got on the bus at the next stop. We got off at the corner of Wenceslas Square. I wanted to accompany him when I suddenly spotted a beautiful mulatto. I hardly had any time to say goodbye to Honzl, but even though I left him so abruptly that he burst into laughter, the mulatto woman had disappeared from sight. Because I thought she had entered the ASO department store, I went in as well and walked past the soap section. To my chagrin, the mulatto woman had truly vanished into thin air. I returned to Wenceslas Square after a quick stop at a publishing house. I would say it was truly the first day of spring. I paused in front of a stationery shop in the Stýblo Arcade. Despite my rather dismal financial situation and almost against my will I ended up buying a fountain pen and had it filled with red ink which, I felt, corresponded very well with the green ink of my older fountain pen. I also bought a leather-bound journal. I went into the New Theater where Honzl was rehearsing the trench scene from *The Treasure of the Jesuits*. And while the rehearsal was entertaining, I was depressed at the thought that I was sitting inside a chilly auditorium on such a beautiful spring day. I walked down Vodičkova Street to the Mánes terraces and wrote "Afternoon Without Memory." Štyrský, who stayed behind with Honzl at the rehearsal, and I were both in the mood this day to treat people rudely and provoke the ladies. Štyrský came up with the idea of going to the Grand Operetta that night. Once there, we amused ourselves by critically commenting upon the girls and demonstrating that we were there only for their nudity. After the show a certain Mr. W. sought me out in the café to arrange a lecture with me. This was the second person of that name to have come into my life in the past few days. The other day it was a Mr. W. who was spreading an ugly rumor about me. He got into a scuffle with some person in a bar and got slapped.

•

During the night of May 6–7 I had this dream:

I do not know why, but the apartment is so crowded that everyone has to sleep in pairs. My girlfriend will sleep with my sister. Me next to them on the other double bed. I'm secretly hoping for the maid to sleep next to me. Surprisingly my mother gives her consent. While I'm rather awkwardly making love to the maid, I learn from her that she used to work for a French friend of mine while he had a wife, about whom he wrote in a book that I love. This coincidence fascinates me all the more when, in my dream, I realize I've met the maid who worked for him once before, when he was married to the woman he mentions elsewhere. Four maids in all, all from Moravia, all working for him, that seems sublime to me. I tell him so. He remembers the last one and calls her Louisa. I have a feeling he ended up firing all four of them. I also realize in my dream that "coincidences" have managed to infiltrate me and my dream. Then I dream that my godfather died. Shortly thereafter I find out that Honzl is dying. There's a dispute over who will succeed him as director. I say indignantly, "Honzl only had what he managed to take, to grab for himself, he never got anything from anyone." I see Honzl, who is about to die. He looks surprisingly hardy, and I can't believe he's going to die. I'm also clearly aware of the terrible situation that awaits his wife and son.

•

The details of these dreams escape me because I only wrote them down in the morning, not right after I woke up. The maid sprung into being from a model who had performed half-naked at the Grand

55

Operetta. My godfather came into the dream from something an eighty-five-year-old lady said to me the other day, "Back then, there were godfathers and uncles left and right." Yesterday, Honzl was wearing a heavy dark coat and black hat, even though it was warm, which compelled me to joke in the arcade to the New Theater: "The director and his black hat play the role of death on this spring day."

•

We sent out the *Bulletin international du surréalisme* to the addresses Paul Éluard gave us. Not long ago I received a letter from H. Bousquet from Carcassonne, who is apparently terminally ill and never leaves his room. He would like to buy Toyen's *Yellow Specter*, for, as he wrote, a yellow ghost has been appearing to him in that very shape and form for some time, which has always foreshadowed catastrophe.

•

Given that André Breton considered the town hall, crocodile, and bicycle I once pointed out to him on our way from the Brno Train Station a chance encounter, a marvelous encounter à la Lautréamont, and given that he and Paul Éluard considered the house signs on Prague's Úvoz Street, where I took them, extremely intriguing Surrealist objects with latent sexual significance, this can only underscore the idea that Surrealism, the discoverer of the human being, will be the discoverer of the manifold marvelous in reality and of the poetics of cities, destroyed by the idiocies of national heritage bureaucrats.

So at the entrance to the Jewish Museum, Éluard, Toyen, and I experienced one of the most truly marvelous situations. After we had inscribed the guest book, displayed there for that purpose and revealed to us by a puppet-like young man, gesturing awkwardly, whom we took to be a deaf mute, as we browsed the museum's wonderful flotsam, our guide made no effort to show us around, unlike those at the cemetery and the Old-New Synagogue, nor offer us a single word of commentary (confirming our impression that he was mute, or, may he forgive us . . .), and when it seemed we were out of earshot of all but the centuries-old walls, this boy, whom we'd already forgotten, said in a high falsetto something I will never forget: Surrealists.

What does it matter if we discovered later who this curious young man was, where he could have known us from, and that it wasn't too difficult for him to name so many of my books starting with *The Jewish Cemetery*; what does the eventual explanation of this miracle matter, an explanation actually very simple and by no means surprising to those of us who do not know and have never known anything about miracles in the metaphysical sense — despite this explanation, the miracle stayed a miracle in the poetic sense, because even before it could be explained, it ignited in us, no matter how brief a moment in space, time, and causality, an eternal flame, so that as we were leaving the old Jewish Quarter in the direction of Old Town Square, all three of us were certain that this person we had met was Isaac Laquedem, who joined Guillaume Apollinaire as he made the rounds of Prague's dive bars, whom Apollinaire saw collapse on the street, and for whom an old Jew rent his garment.

And if I add that more than fourteen days before this incident occurred I wrote these three lines of automatic text:

> *At the last moment*
> *Isaac Laquedem*
> *In a Gothic window*

which, oddly enough, brought everything that day to a close for me, I cannot help but suggest a connection between this unfinished automatic text, which I immediately analyzed in amazement that it ended so prematurely, and the incident that ended in March 1902 with Apollinaire's "passant de Prague" manically exclaiming as he collapsed to the ground: "Thank you. The time has come. Every ninety to a hundred years I am stricken by a terrible illness, but I survive, and discover that I have the strength for another century of living," who in April 1935 addressed us in a child's voice, saying one single word: Surrealists.

3

AFTERNOON WITHOUT MEMORY

1.

An umbrella woman paddles on divan fortifications
Of a Thursday at four-thirty when
Airless Prague flies south

2.

I asked a seahorse
Is it better to dry up like a leaf or to ruin our most fascinating hours
By our desire to perpetuate them
And the cuttlefish replied
I weep red ink that's all

3.

No matter how deeply I might look
Into the eyes of all the women of this hothouse afternoon
I will not come across anything so grand
To make me choose it over the silent indolence
Of the sun
For over a year I waited for you
And all just so my pen and I could someday go outside
To the terrace where all beautiful women feel embarrassed
Just so I could shed a tear over all that waiting
Over the pleasure of the unknown rubbing against me like a cat
Just for two or three words of hope or despair

4.

And still it is beautiful to speak to nameless creatures
More beautiful than speaking to women
And most beautiful of all is to regret life
Since it has always slipped through our fingers
Most when we thought it had become our prey
Least when we suffered that it gave us nothing

5.

I love the allure of despair
More skittish than a bird a soft track
I will never step on and yet
Goodbye or farewell little nothing

6.

I wrote only for the pleasure of handwriting
I kept silent only for the bitterness of silence
And yet the one happiness I know
Is that headlong cyclist gaining on night

7.

The sun shines a woman sings and a bird
Traces a prophecy in the sky
That does not concern me
Just like the sun like the bird like the woman

Farewell sun
In a moment you'll be gone like a date on a calendar
Whose pages I tear off
Searching for the sun and not finding the woman

This voice inducing me
To fall into step with who's singing
And enter the house as the sun sets through its windows
Is a street organ

So life flee like this smile
Or like I flee from myself
Seeing only a terribly long shadow on even longer biers
And the scent of carnation that accompanies a meteor burning out

8.

I wanted little in life I hardly wanted anything
But a few days of aimless sunlight
To which I surrender my meager hopes
Like a rainbow to a soused garden
But had I wanted even less
Had I wanted nothing save what I've received
It would be enough to bring joy to this entire café
Over which this year's spring appeared to me

4

THE BIRD OF DOOM

Brief Prologue

The front curtain rises. Two sacks sit in front of the rear curtain. Silence. An OLD COUNTRYWOMAN enters. She is carrying a full basket of potatoes. She reaches down three times or so. She shakes out the potatoes into one of the sacks, which is already nearly full. She ties the sack, and then unties the other to pour the rest of the potatoes into it. The BIRD OF DOOM emerges from the sack. The old woman shrieks, crosses herself, drops her basket of potatoes, and flees the scene. The BIRD OF DOOM steps out of the sack and stretches his limbs.

Curtain

A vestibule. Coatracks. Dimly lit. Red cue light. Small fan. Silence. A CHAMBERMAID *enters, carrying several men's and women's hats and coats draped over her arm. She carefully arranges them on the coatracks to make them look as picturesque as possible. She moves a hat from the third coatrack to the fifth. Then she changes her mind and places it on the second. She fixes her hair in front of a mirror. The doorbell rings.*

CHAMBERMAID: (*Goes to open the door. A* NEURASTHENIC WOMAN *enters. The* CHAMBERMAID *bows to her. The* NEURASTHENIC WOMAN *looks around, then pulls a slip of paper out of her purse and hands it to the* CHAMBERMAID.) Thank you.

NEURASTHENIC WOMAN: (*her eyes fixed on the second coatrack*) Who is that man?

CHAMBERMAID: (*shrugs and deposits the ticket into the box*)

NEURASTHENIC WOMAN: I'll come back later.

CHAMBERMAID: Pardon me, but the tickets are non-refundable.

NEURASTHENIC WOMAN: And if I leave?

CHAMBERMAID: The ticket is void.

NEURASTHENIC WOMAN: What's going to happen in there?

CHAMBERMAID: I don't know. I'm just the chambermaid. Let me take your coat. (*The doorbell rings.*) Hold on. Here's the waiting room. (*The* NEURASTHENIC WOMAN *enters the waiting room. The* CHAMBERMAID *lets in a* YOUNG MAN. *She bows him in. The* YOUNG MAN *quickly sheds his overcoat and throws it over the* CHAMBERMAID's *arm.*) The gentleman's ticket, please?

YOUNG MAN: Of course. (*He pulls out his ticket. The* NEURAS-THENIC WOMAN *enters.*)

CHAMBERMAID: One moment, please. (*She deposits the ticket into the box.*)

NEURASTHENIC WOMAN: I was here first.

YOUNG MAN: I'll wait.

NEURASTHENIC WOMAN: Never mind. Just go in.

YOUNG MAN: (*puts on his coat*) I'll come back later.

NEURASTHENIC WOMAN: Your ticket will be void.

YOUNG MAN: I've changed my mind about the whole thing. Sorry . . . (*He leaves.*)

NEURASTHENIC WOMAN: Who are these ladies? (*She points to a coatrack.*)

CHAMBERMAID: I don't recall.

NEURASTHENIC WOMAN: How unhelpful! Goodbye. (*She exits.*)

CHAMBERMAID: (*Dusts in the lobby. The doorbell rings. A* FAT GENTLEMAN *enters.*)

FAT GENTLEMAN: (*takes off his overcoat*) I'm surprised there's no elevator.

CHAMBERMAID: Does the gentleman have a ticket?

FAT GENTLEMAN: I came because of the advertisement.

CHAMBERMAID: The entrance fee is usually sent in advance by mail.

FAT GENTLEMAN: I spotted the ad just a little while ago in a café.

CHAMBERMAID: All right. The entry fee is one hundred crowns. Refreshments are not included.

FAT GENTLEMAN: I just wanted to use the baths.

CHAMBERMAID: The baths?

FAT GENTLEMAN: What is the hundred crowns for then?

CHAMBERMAID: Pardon, but I'm just the chambermaid.

FAT GENTLEMAN: And these ladies? (*He points to a coatrack.*)

CHAMBERMAID: I don't know. No one introduces themselves here.

FAT GENTLEMAN: It's starting to make sense.

CHAMBERMAID: Would the gentleman like to purchase a ticket?

FAT GENTLEMAN: I'll come back later. I didn't count on the extra expense. (*The doorbell rings.*)

CHAMBERMAID: Excuse me! Here's the waiting room. (*She leads the* FAT GENTLEMAN *to the waiting room, closes the door behind him, and goes to open the other door.*)

HILDA: (*enters, hands over her ticket without a word, does not ask any questions or look around, takes off her coat, and walks through the door the* CHAMBERMAID *shows her*)

FAT GENTLEMAN: (*Leaves the waiting room just as* HILDA *disappears behind the door and manages to catch a glimpse of her. As he speaks, he inadvertently touches* HILDA's *coat, smelling of her perfume.*) How late are you open, miss?

CHAMBERMAID: We never close, sir.

FAT GENTLEMAN: I'll be back in a moment. Here's something for your troubles, miss.

CHAMBERMAID: Thank you, sir. (*She deposits the tip into the box.*)

FAT GENTLEMAN: So long, miss.

CHAMBERMAID: Goodbye, sir.

FAT GENTLEMAN: (*exits after a moment of hesitation*)

CHAMBERMAID: (*Takes one of the women's coats and returns at the sound of the doorbell to let in a young couple. A* TWENTY-YEAR-OLD MAN *enters, followed by a* TWENTY-YEAR-OLD WOMAN *who seems quite uneasy.*) Come in, please.

TWENTY-YEAR-OLD MAN: (*looking around*) It's already packed.

CHAMBERMAID: Tickets, please.

TWENTY-YEAR-OLD MAN: I want to see the house rules.

CHAMBERMAID: I don't follow, sir.

TWENTY-YEAR-OLD MAN: The program.

CHAMBERMAID: There isn't one, sir.

TWENTY-YEAR-OLD MAN: But I would like to know what I've paid for.

CHAMBERMAID: Everything will be clear once you're inside.

TWENTY-YEAR-OLD MAN: Let's go in then.

TWENTY-YEAR-OLD WOMAN: Wait, wait a minute.

TWENTY-YEAR-OLD MAN: Having second thoughts?

TWENTY-YEAR-OLD WOMAN: No, but ...

CHAMBERMAID: May I see your tickets?

TWENTY-YEAR-OLD MAN: Here you are. (*He produces the tickets, the* CHAMBERMAID *deposits them into the box.*)

CHAMBERMAID: May I take your coat, ma'am?

TWENTY-YEAR-OLD WOMAN: No, I'm cold. (*To her companion.*) Will we be alone?

TWENTY-YEAR-OLD MAN: Do you know?

CHAMBERMAID: I'm just the chambermaid, sir.

TWENTY-YEAR-OLD MAN: Let's go.

TWENTY-YEAR-OLD WOMAN: (*bursts into tears*)

TWENTY-YEAR-OLD MAN: I'll go in by myself then.

TWENTY-YEAR-OLD WOMAN: (*tosses back her head and stops crying*) Could I get some writing paper and an envelope, miss?

CHAMBERMAID: You will find everything inside.

TWENTY-YEAR-OLD WOMAN: Thank you. (*She clutches her companion and they go through the door the* CHAMBERMAID *shows them. The* CHAMBERMAID *closes the door behind them. A moment of silence. Suddenly, the door the couple went through flies open. The* TWENTY-YEAR-OLD WOMAN, *in tears, dashes down the hallway, a terrified* TWENTY-YEAR-OLD MAN *hot on her heels. They rush outside.*)

CHAMBERMAID: (*Closes the door behind the fleeing couple when the doorbell rings again. A* MADE-UP WOMAN *enters.*)

MADE-UP WOMAN: (*Hands over her ticket and coat. She looks into the mirror, fixes her hat, and walks to the door pointed out by the* CHAMBERMAID.) What's today's date?

CHAMBERMAID: July 18, ma'am.

MADE-UP WOMAN: Thank you. (*She enters.*)

CHAMBERMAID: (*Returns to the door. The doorbell rings. Three men enter:* GASTON, *a* WIDOWER, *and a* COCAINE ADDICT. *Without a word, they present their tickets, take off their jackets, and, making way for one another, go inside. Once they are gone, the* CHAMBERMAID *takes from a coatrack some of the coats and hats from the first arrivals, draping them over her arm, and brings them into the waiting room.*)

OWNER: (*Enters from inside, glances at his watch impatiently, then at the coatracks. He walks over to the telephone, dials a number, says nothing, and hangs up. The doorbell rings. The* OWNER *goes to the door and opens it. The* BIRD OF DOOM *enters at the same time as the*

CHAMBERMAID. *The* OWNER *signals for her to leave.*) I've been expecting you. We have a full house.

BIRD OF DOOM: I can see that . . . (*He glances at the coatracks.*)

OWNER: What now?

BIRD OF DOOM: Hard to say in advance.

OWNER: This was your idea, after all.

BIRD OF DOOM: My idea was good. Rounding up as many guests as possible to pay a rather high price of admission.

OWNER: What do we do with them now?

BIRD OF DOOM: Let them enjoy themselves.

OWNER: Somebody has to start.

BIRD OF DOOM: Somebody will.

OWNER: I thought you had a specific program in mind.

BIRD OF DOOM: A specific program? It doesn't work that way. I think that a select group has come. We can be certain of that. Actually, let's make sure right away. (*He goes from coat to coat and digs through the pockets. One by one he pulls six revolvers from the pockets.*) What do you say to that?

OWNER: It's quite disturbing. What do you think?

BIRD OF DOOM: Yes, just a bit.

OWNER: The ad's wording is questionable.

BIRD OF DOOM: I'm proud of it.

OWNER: (*reads aloud from a newspaper*) Before you take your last step in life, visit The Pessimists' Club.

BIRD OF DOOM: It's perfect, don't you think?

OWNER: So what happens now?

BIRD OF DOOM: The ad isn't binding in any way. And you do have a liquor license for an entertainment venue.

OWNER: Some fun, hosting the suicidal. (*The doorbell rings.*) Excuse me! (*He goes to open the door. The* FAT GENTLEMAN *enters.*)

FAT GENTLEMAN: I was here before. Here's the fee.

OWNER: Thank you, sir.

FAT GENTLEMAN: I would like to bathe.

OWNER: Right this way.

FAT GENTLEMAN: Introduce me.

OWNER: I'm afraid it's not customary here.

FAT GENTLEMAN: (*points at* HILDA's *coat*) To this one . . .

OWNER: The group is inside.

FAT GENTLEMAN: I'm not the sociable type.

OWNER: (*leads him to the door*) This way, please.

FAT GENTLEMAN: I want to go straight to the baths.

OWNER: One moment, sir. (*He rings a bell. The* CHAMBERMAID *enters.*) Prepare a bath.

CHAMBERMAID: Yes, sir. (*She leaves.*)

FAT GENTLEMAN: You should have an elevator here. (*He goes inside.*)

OWNER: A suspicious-looking fellow. I won't let him into the baths.

BIRD OF DOOM: We'll find out soon enough. (*He searches the* FAT GENTLEMAN's *overcoat and pulls out a salami.*) Just as I thought. He thinks the club is a massage parlor.

OWNER: That's not the worst of it. Unfortunately, he's the only one who read the ad in a sober frame of mind.

BIRD OF DOOM: An optimist. Just like the rest of them. Otherwise, they wouldn't have come.

OWNER: Why did they come?

BIRD OF DOOM: We'll see.

CHAMBERMAID: (*enters, distraught*) Sir, I am sorry, but I simply cannot stay here a second longer.

OWNER: Why not, miss?

CHAMBERMAID: You asked me to prepare the bath. When I entered the spa . . . (*She is panting nervously.*)

OWNER: Did the fat gentleman harass you?

CHAMBERMAID: (*in one breath*) I smelled gas coming from one of the cabins. I looked through a crack and saw a person in the tub who's probably dead. It's one of them. This one! (*She points to a coatrack.*) And anyway, it seems to me everyone who's come here is crazy.

OWNER: Close off the gas main and come with me. (*He leaves with the* BIRD OF DOOM.)

CHAMBERMAID: (*Turns the gas main's lever. All of the lights go out. Only a small red bulb glows over the door. The stage is empty.*)

GASTON: (*Enters the hallway, smoking a cigarette. He tosses it and looks closely into the pitch-black mirror. He takes a deep breath and saunters over to the coatracks. He feels around in his coat pocket and pulls out a revolver. The sound of the gun cocking is heard. At the same time, the* CHAMBERMAID *walks in, hat and coat on, and as* GASTON *is raising the revolver, the* CHAMBERMAID *grabs his arm.* GASTON *lowers his arm, the* CHAMBERMAID *takes the revolver from his hand and puts it in her bag.*) Thank you.

CHAMBERMAID: Has someone hurt you? . . . Thousands of people have hurt me. Farewell, sir, and may your life take a turn for the better.

GASTON: Who are you?

CHAMBERMAID: A woman. Like any other.

GASTON: (*takes the* CHAMBERMAID'*s head in his hands, stares into her eyes, and then kisses her*) I suddenly feel okay. (*He exits with the* CHAMBERMAID.)

Curtain

The front curtain rises. A large white crinkled bedsheet can be seen in front of the rear curtain, concealing a figure. The melody of a distant harmonica is heard. In front of the shrouded figure is a miniature red light, the kind used to signal road construction ahead. A rooster crows in the distance.

Curtain

The Bird of Doom is born
Like a day with hewed roots
The festivity on its branches
Tumbles down like a toy chest
The wind of black cloth
Rages through every mousehole
The sun a gigantic burning sprig
Burns out in a pool of its own blood
An immense wheel that drives the mill of sibyls
Is witness to a great lamentation
Of fowl on the fire
Made of the canvas of molded terrain
The Bird of Doom is born
Like a blacksmith's forge grown dim
As the leg falls asleep during a lullaby
While night opens its gigantic forest
The Bird of Doom is born
Like straw in a blaze
When a meteor in flight
Said its *forever* right over the horizon
The Bird of Doom is born
Like a dazed morning thought
Coming to drink
From the breast of the bell that has awakened it

A counter separates the interior of the pawnshop from the customers. Two staff at work: an APPRAISER *and a* CASHIER. *The interior of the pawnshop is full of junk. About six people are in the customer section, most of them in front of the* APPRAISER's *window. The* TWENTY-YEAR-OLD MAN *is next in line.*

APPRAISER: (*to an* ELDERLY WOMAN) We don't purchase here, we just take items as collateral.

ELDERLY WOMAN: What about a bracelet?

APPRAISER: You want to get rid of it?

ELDERLY WOMAN: I need the money.

APPRAISER: I can't just buy any piece of jewelry. Where did you get it?

ELDERLY WOMAN: I had a tenant, an actress. She owes me rent . . .

APPRAISER: Thirty crowns.

ELDERLY WOMAN: She said it cost sixteen hundred.

APPRAISER: Pay back the thirty crowns within six months and the bracelet is yours.

ELDERLY WOMAN: But I thought that . . .

APPRAISER: You want it or not?

ELDERLY WOMAN: I'm not sure . . .

APPRAISER: We're about to close. Make up your mind already.

ELDERLY WOMAN: Why would I want to keep it anyway?

APPRAISER: You'll be paid the thirty crowns at the next window.

ELDERLY WOMAN: Pawn it, they said . . . Fast money, they said . . . (*She goes to the next window. The* TWENTY-YEAR-OLD MAN *is next in line, but a* MAN WITH A PIPE *cuts in front.*)

MAN WITH A PIPE: Pardon me, sir, I'm in a hurry to catch a train. (*To the* APPRAISER.) Here. (*He shows him a ring.*)

APPRAISER: A new one is worth ten, fifteen crowns. We're not interested.

MAN WITH A PIPE: Goodbye then. (*He leaves. In the meantime, the* CASHIER *has paid out thirty crowns to the* ELDERLY WOMAN. *He closes his window and goes to the* APPRAISER.)

CASHIER: I've got to run. Cover for me.

APPRAISER: (*with a smile*) Say hello to . . . and (*he whispers something in the* CASHIER'*s ear, and then speaks to the crowd*). Ladies and gentlemen, don't always leave it to the last minute.

TWENTY-YEAR-OLD MAN: (*quietly*) Excuse me, do you accept . . . guns?

APPRAISER: What kind?

TWENTY-YEAR-OLD MAN: (*whispers something*)

APPRAISER: A Browning? Let's see it. But careful, careful . . .

TWENTY-YEAR-OLD MAN: (*Slips his hand into his pocket. Then starts digging through all his pockets, becoming more and more agitated.*) I had it right here, I'm sure of it. (*He keeps searching.*)

APPRAISER: Easy, take it easy.

TWENTY-YEAR-OLD MAN: I was holding it just a second ago.

APPRAISER: A Browning doesn't vanish just like that.

TWENTY-YEAR-OLD MAN: Someone's robbed me.

APPRAISER: Watch your pockets! It's printed here on one, two, three, four signs ...

TWENTY-YEAR-OLD MAN: It cost three hundred crowns and was never fired.

APPRAISER: What can I do?

TWENTY-YEAR-OLD MAN: Goodbye.

ATTENDANT: Closing time! (*The* BIRD OF DOOM *enters. He walks to the* APPRAISER's *window.*)

APPRAISER: (*to the* ATTENDANT) Bring the key here and you can go. (*Nervously, as if to himself.*) What's today's date?

BIRD OF DOOM: July 19.

APPRAISER: I've written it today a hundred times already ... What have you got?

BIRD OF DOOM: Two rings and a pair of earrings.

APPRAISER: Hold on. (*He examines the jewelry with a magnifying glass.*) Sixty-five crowns for the lot.

ATTENDANT: (*hands the key to the* APPRAISER) Have a nice evening.

BIRD OF DOOM: All right.

APPRAISER: Pick up the collars for me on Monday. (*He hands the* ATTENDANT *a sales slip.*)

ATTENDANT: Okay. (*He exits.*)

APPRAISER: What price did I quote you?

BIRD OF DOOM: Sixty-five crowns.

APPRAISER: (*counting out the money*) Oh, I'm so scatterbrained today.

BIRD OF DOOM: No wonder. Farewell. (*He exits.*)

APPRAISER: (*Lights a cigarette and stands up to sharpen his pencil. He is very morose.*)

HILDA: (*barges in and shuts the door behind her*) Sir, I apologize for seeking your help. I was being followed on the street by a man who stopped me and made veiled threats. It's clearly some sort of mix-up. I managed to lose him at the street corner, and I feared he might spot me again, so I came in here, thinking it was the post office.

APPRAISER: I'll call the police. Please come in, ma'am.

HILDA: I don't think it will be necessary to involve the police. May I? (*She wants to enter.*)

APPRAISER: (*opens the door for her*) Take a seat, ma'am.

HILDA: Thank you, sir. You are too kind. Oh, what lovely jewelry!

APPRAISER: They are for sale at a very low price.

HILDA: Now I see that I'm in a pawnshop. I was so distraught before.

APPRAISER: Normally we would be closed by now. Today, ahead of Sunday, we were busier than usual. And thanks to this circumstance I'm able to make your acquaintance.

HILDA: I can see that I'm keeping you.

APPRAISER: Not at all. As you can see, I'm having a smoke. Would you care for one?

HILDA: (*takes a cigarette*) Thank you.

APPRAISER: That chair is all dusty. Take mine instead.

HILDA: (*sits down*) Which piece of jewelry should I appraise? You won't laugh, will you?

APPRAISER: Women have a better instinct for appraising valuables than those of us who employ objective methods.

HILDA: What an exquisite bracelet.

APPRAISER: It belonged to some actress and was pawned by her landlady.

HILDA: Would it by chance be for sale?

APPRAISER: Not for another six months, if it's not redeemed. I have only myself to blame. I could have had it for very cheap.

HILDA: I don't wear jewelry. I could never stand to have a ring on my finger.

APPRAISER: A marvelous hand. (*He kisses Hilda's hand.*) Marvelous fingers.

HILDA: Why have you gone so pale?

APPRAISER: (*throws away his cigarette*) Smoking doesn't agree with me. I have to spend nearly the whole day in this terrible air.

HILDA: I hope my pursuer is no longer lurking about. I think it's safe for me to leave now. Thank you, sir.

APPRAISER: May I accompany you?

HILDA: Thank you, but I always walk alone.

APPRAISER: What if I kept an eye on you from a distance?

HILDA: The sound of footsteps behind me terrifies me.

APPRAISER: So I'll walk a few steps ahead of you.

HILDA: That would please me. You are very kind.

APPRAISER: As soon as I put away this jewelry. May I see your hand once more?

HILDA: Farewell, sir. (*She extends her arm. The* APPRAISER *fastens the bracelet on it.*) Sir, what are you doing . . .

APPRAISER: A little souvenir.

HILDA: The bracelet is in hock. Control yourself.

APPRAISER: I will easily replace it with something similar.

HILDA: I cannot accept this.

APPRAISER: No, you mustn't leave just yet. I haven't shown you everything. There's jewelry worth hundreds of thousands of crowns in this case. Give me your pocketbook. By tomorrow we could be on the other side of the world. Across the ocean . . .

HILDA: Farewell, sir. This really is unseemly of you.

APPRAISER: The thought has never crossed my mind before. How easy it seems to commit a crime out of the blue.

HILDA: Yes, it is very easy.

APPRAISER: Those hands, those hands!

HILDA: Were they created merely for the purpose of stealing? Where have I heard that before! What a foolish saying. Take off this manacle!

APPRAISER: (*removes the bracelet*) You'll wear one even more beautiful.

HILDA: Never, sir.

APPRAISER: I'll show you the treasure trove. (*He tries different keys.*)

HILDA: I hate jewels. What on earth is wrong with you?

APPRAISER: I love you.

HILDA: (*laughs loudly*) What an idiotic way to unlock the case! A thief you'll never be.

APPRAISER: The cashier didn't leave the key. He doesn't trust me.

HILDA: And for good reason.

APPRAISER: It never occurred to me before, that I could . . . Besides, you're right, this is madness.

HILDA: To steal for a woman like me, eh?

APPRAISER: I love you. I love you. Oh, if only I had the key ... I feel so powerless!

HILDA: This is how you pick a lock. And then it's goodbye ... (*She inserts a thin needle into the lock, her fingers performing intricate movements.*)

APPRAISER: You? ... You? ... Ah, those hands.

HILDA: You want to see your treasure? Patience, patience ...

APPRAISER: It must be madness after all.

HILDA: (*opens the case full of glittering jewels*)

APPRAISER: Who are you?

HILDA: A woman. A woman like any other. (*She walks right up to the* APPRAISER *and looks him in the eye.*)

APPRAISER: (*takes her into his arms and bends down to kiss her*) It surely must be madness ...

HILDA: Madness? ... Yes, madness. (*She lets him kiss her, slips her hands from his; performing intricate movements, her fingers touch his temples as they kiss, run down his cheeks, caress his neck, then squeeze it and frantically strangle him. The* APPRAISER'S *legs give way and he suddenly drops to the ground.* HILDA *walks into the light and gazes wordlessly at her hands. She walks past the open case with the jewels, glances at them with disdain, and leaves without touching anything. As she reaches for the latch to open the door, the door opens on its own and the* MAN WITH A PIPE *gingerly enters. Because he doesn't shut the door,* HILDA *stays concealed behind it.*)

MAN WITH A PIPE: (*walks up to the* APPRAISER'S *window*)

HILDA: (*deftly slips out the door and disappears*)

MAN WITH A PIPE: (*Peers through the open counter window into the pawnshop and spots the* APPRAISER's *body lying on the floor. He quickly goes in, and as he is bending over the body the open jewelry case catches his eye. He expertly inspects the way the lock was picked. Then, as if smelling a familiar perfume in the air.*) So Hilda was here . . . (*He reaches into the case and touches the jewels.*)

TWENTY-YEAR-OLD MAN: (*noisily enters the pawnshop with a* POLICEMAN) No one else could have stolen the Browning except him. He was standing right behind me.

POLICEMAN: The shop is already closed.

MAN WITH A PIPE: (*slowly closes the jewelry case and walks toward the* POLICEMAN, *pointing the gun at him*) Out of the way!

TWENTY-YEAR-OLD MAN: Don't worry, Officer, it's not loaded. I recognize my Browning.

MAN WITH A PIPE: (*throws down the revolver and tries to flee*)

POLICEMAN: (*jumps on him and handcuffs him*)

Curtain

The front curtain rises. The rear curtain rises. An empty room. Three paintings on the walls. In the center of the room is a sewing machine in motion. The first painting falls to the ground. After an interval, the second and third paintings also fall. The sewing machine keeps spinning out its white fabric.

Curtain

The Bird of Doom flies
Like the innocence of a quilt
From an overheated bed
Of a woman tattooed with dread
This slumber on a footbridge
Anxiously evades the half-turn
That ends everything
Like the skid of a star
Of sea land hardship
Pride indifference and naked life itself
Will be part of the crash
Of two cymbals furiously cast
Into a well with a wandering echo
And the Bird of Doom flies forth
Like a funeral announcement
Or like the scent of jasmine
No chamomile
Can allay
Like a city hurled into the air
Because of a desperate rupture
In thoughts that pointlessly sew
A tablecloth of charred hope

In the Dressing Room

A simple theater dressing room. The lights are still turned off. A huge mess everywhere.

BIRD OF DOOM: (*Enters and turns on the light. He is carrying a basket of flowers and places them in front of the mirror. He tidies up the scattered chairs and exits.*)

YOUNG ACTRESS: (*knocks on the door before entering*) Ema . . . Ema! (*She enters and looks around. She leans over the basket of flowers and picks up one of three identical wigs.*)

ELDERLY WOMAN: (*knocks and enters*) Good evening, miss.

YOUNG ACTRESS: Can I help you?

ELDERLY WOMAN: Is Miss Ema here?

YOUNG ACTRESS: Miss Ema?

ELDERLY WOMAN: I'm her landlady.

YOUNG ACTRESS: She's not here yet. Can I give her a message?

ELDERLY WOMAN: I'll wait. (*A bell rings.*)

YOUNG ACTRESS: That's the call. She should be here by now. (*A knock on the door.*)

OLD LADY: (*enters*)

YOUNG ACTRESS: May I help you?

OLD LADY: I've come to see my daughter.

YOUNG ACTRESS: Please take a seat. Ema should be here any minute.

OLD LADY: I'll wait.

YOUNG ACTRESS: I'll see you later. (*Exits.*)

ELDERLY WOMAN: I didn't know Ema had a mother. She never mentioned you.

OLD LADY: No?

ELDERLY WOMAN: I'm her landlady.

OLD LADY: Oh?

ELDERLY WOMAN: She roomed at my place for over a year.

OLD LADY: Over a year . . .

ELDERLY WOMAN: And then one day she just up and left. I'm not even sure where. Well, that's actresses for you.

OLD LADY: Yes . . .

ELDERLY WOMAN: I still have some of her jewelry.

OLD LADY: Jewelry?

ELDERLY WOMAN: I pawned it.

OLD LADY: Pawned?

ELDERLY WOMAN: I'd like to return it to her.

OLD LADY: Oh?

ELDERLY WOMAN: Must've gotten held up somewhere.

OLD LADY: Let's hope she makes it.

ELDERLY WOMAN: Have you come a long way?

OLD LADY: A long way.

DIRECTOR: (*enters with two men*) I'm very surprised, gentlemen, she hasn't shown up yet.

FIRST MAN: Who are these women?

OLD LADY: I'm her mother.

FIRST MAN: Do you live around here?

OLD LADY: I've come a long way to see my daughter.

FIRST MAN: And you?

ELDERLY WOMAN: I'm her landlady.

FIRST MAN: Damn, how many apartments does she keep?

ELDERLY WOMAN: I mean, her former landlady. She hasn't paid her rent.

OLD LADY: Oh?

DIRECTOR: She should be here any minute. She's on in the fifth scene of Act I.

FIRST MAN: We'll conduct the search in her absence.

DIRECTOR: What is this about, gentlemen? As director, I must protest. She is one of our most excellent artists. I don't want my theater to become embroiled in a scandal.

FIRST MAN: We have a search warrant.

DIRECTOR: As you wish, gentlemen.

ELDERLY WOMAN: (*stands up*) Have a good evening. (*She wants to leave.*)

FIRST MAN: What's the hurry?

ELDERLY WOMAN: I don't have time to keep waiting. She might not even show up.

FIRST MAN: Admit it, you're smuggling cocaine!

ELDERLY WOMAN: (*tearfully*) Me? What sort of nonsense is this?

FIRST MAN: Search her!

SECOND MAN: What's that in your pocketbook?

ELDERLY WOMAN: It belongs to her . . .

SECOND MAN: (*searches the pocketbook*) Gold. Where did you get it? And don't lie.

ELDERLY WOMAN: As God is my witness, I have done nothing wrong.

SECOND MAN: And this receipt?

ELDERLY WOMAN: They gave it to me at the pawnshop. (*To the* OLD LADY.) Ma'am, please tell your daughter to pay me the rent. I want nothing to do with her gold. (*She throws the jewelry on the table.*) She can keep it, and if she doesn't pay what she owes, I'll get by without it.

OLD LADY: How much does she owe you?

ELDERLY WOMAN: Twelve hundred.

OLD LADY: Here's at least some of it. (*She looks in her pocketbook, takes out some banknotes, and hands them to the* ELDERLY WOMAN.) You will return the jewelry to her.

ELDERLY WOMAN: Better to tie up loose ends. What bad times we're living in. May I leave now, gentlemen? I have no more business here.

FIRST MAN: Go with her!

SECOND MAN: Okay.

FIRST MAN: Hand me that suitcase over there first.

SECOND MAN: (*takes down a suitcase from the wardrobe*)

FIRST MAN: You can go!

SECOND MAN: Go on. (*He pushes the* ELDERLY WOMAN *through the door and leaves with her.*)

FIRST MAN: (*rummages through the suitcase and after a moment closes it, annoyed*)

DIRECTOR: I don't understand why she isn't here yet. (*A bell rings.*) The performance is starting.

FIRST MAN: (*snooping around*) Know anything about her private life?

DIRECTOR: She keeps to herself.

FIRST MAN: If anything comes up, you'll let me know?

DIRECTOR: You've got her all wrong.

FIRST MAN: I think I'm done with my search. Goodbye.

DIRECTOR: I'll show you out, sir.

FIRST MAN: Forgive me, I'm just doing my job. (*Both men leave.*)

OLD LADY: (*Gets up after they exit, turns off the light, and quickly gets undressed. We soon see that she is a young woman with a beautiful figure. She puts the dress she's been wearing into the basket of flowers. Then she turns on the light. We recognize the* MADE-UP WOMAN. *She opens the wardrobe and takes out a costume. Then she sits in front of the mirror, quickly does her makeup, and takes one of the two identical wigs.*)

DIRECTOR: (*enters the dressing room with the* YOUNG ACTRESS, *who is wearing her wig*) You have to fill in for her. I can't explain it . . . Ah, so you made it?

MADE-UP WOMAN: I was waiting at the station for my mother, who wrote me that she was coming to visit.

DIRECTOR: Isn't she here?

MADE-UP WOMAN: No, nobody was here when I came in. (*A bell rings.*) That's my cue. I'm ready.

DIRECTOR: Next time don't be so late, miss.

MADE-UP WOMAN: I'm truly sorry. (*Exits.*)

DIRECTOR: Don't forget your prop.

MADE-UP WOMAN: (*takes the basket of flowers*) So much rush. (*Exits.*)

DIRECTOR: (*to the* YOUNG ACTRESS) Thank you, miss.

YOUNG ACTRESS: So I can remove my makeup then?

DIRECTOR: Ah, you've already put on the makeup for her role? The wig looks perfect on you.

YOUNG ACTRESS: It seemed like she wasn't going to show up . . .

DIRECTOR: I'm truly grateful to you for having such presence of mind.

YOUNG ACTRESS: Oh, I was really looking forward to performing. (*Applause.*)

DIRECTOR: She's already onstage. Just a moment, I'll have a look. (*He exits the dressing room.*)

YOUNG ACTRESS: (*Walks to the table. A knock at the door. The* YOUNG ACTRESS *pulls a package from her bosom, looks around for a place to put it, then grabs the* MADE-UP WOMAN's *pocketbook, slips the package in, and moves away from the table. Another knock at the door.*) Come in.

NEURASTHENIC WOMAN: (*enters and stands glaring at the* YOUNG ACTRESS)

YOUNG ACTRESS: Can I help you?

NEURASTHENIC WOMAN: You got my letter today. You know full well who I am!

YOUNG ACTRESS: Sorry, Ema is onstage.

NEURASTHENIC WOMAN: You'll answer to me for everything. I swore that today they wouldn't applaud you.

YOUNG ACTRESS: Ah, this is a misunderstanding . . .

NEURASTHENIC WOMAN: Today's the last time you'll be dressed like a vamp.

YOUNG ACTRESS: You're mistaken, madam, I'm not . . .

NEURASTHENIC WOMAN: Your days of addling men's minds with your eyes are over! (*She throws acid into the* YOUNG ACTRESS's *face.*)

YOUNG ACTRESS: (*staggers with a scream*)

NEURASTHENIC WOMAN: (*Stares at her as if transfixed. She drops the vial and flees, leaving the door open.*)

YOUNG ACTRESS: (*Staggers to the table with the expression of a blinded person, fumbling around until she grasps the pocketbook. She rifles through it, pulling out the package and holding it to her breast.*) Ema . . . Ema . . . Forgive me. I'm a woman like any other. (*She falls to the floor. The applause audible through the open door grows louder.*)

Curtain

3RD INTERLUDE

The front curtain rises. In front of the rear curtain, a cask girded with two wreaths sits on a rocking chair covered in roses. Red liquid is flowing from the spigot of the cask into a women's welly boot while the second boot lies on the floor. The melody of a musical clock accompanies the scene.

Curtain

The Bird of Doom smokes a pipe
Like other beings lose themselves in prayer
His wounded eye
Searches for a lost thimble
The mushroom he sits on
Resembles a Christmas sky
Jagged by the restless flames
Of resinated tobacco sparks
Like the lice tormenting him
He squeezes in his handkerchief
The war cry of kisses
That suddenly falls silent when
The human scent from the chimney opposite
Lulls his conscience
That made him rub his eyes
Like other beings surrender to love

The Woods

A clearing in the woods, with an enormous anthill in the middle. Dusk is falling.

DAY-TRIPPERS: (*returning from a typical Sunday outing, singing, a harmonica, jabbering*)

FAT GENTLEMAN: (*walking with his wife and two children, wearing plus fours and a backpack*) I can't take another step.

MISSUS: We'll be out of the woods in fifteen minutes.

FAT GENTLEMAN: I'm hungry. Sit down, children. Would be a waste to just lug it all back home.

LITTLE GIRL: I'm sleepy, Daddy.

MISSUS: Give her a little coffee.

FAT GENTLEMAN: Here's an orange.

MISSUS: She'll get a stomachache.

FAT GENTLEMAN: Want a piece of salami?

MISSUS: Just the thought of you eating it makes me nauseous.

FAT GENTLEMAN: We've walked too much.

LITTLE GIRL: Mommy, something itches.

MISSUS: Get up, we're right next to an anthill, look.

BOY: Wow, look at that heap . . .

FAT GENTLEMAN: Where?

BOY: (*running to the anthill*) There's so many of them . . .

FAT GENTLEMAN: I've lost my knife.

MISSUS: You jabbed it into the ground back by those tree stumps.

BOY: What if I pour coffee on them?

MISSUS: Get over here at once.

FAT GENTLEMAN: Should we go back for the knife?

MISSUS: You go. We'll wait for you at the edge of the woods.

LITTLE GIRL: Mommy, I'm sleepy.

MISSUS: Next time we're not going anywhere.

BOY: (*kicks the anthill*)

MISSUS: You rascal! You'll get a shoeful of ants! Get over here at once.

FAT GENTLEMAN: Let's get a move on. (*He has trouble getting up.*)

MISSUS: Don't take long!

FAT GENTLEMAN: Goddamn Sunday . . . (*He goes back into the woods.*)

MISSUS: Get away from that anthill! Or we'll leave you here.

BOY: (*running off*) I'll be the first one to the road!

MISSUS: You want me to carry you? You're about to nod off . . . Oh, that daddy of yours! (*She picks up the* LITTLE GIRL *and walks off.*)

BIRD OF DOOM: (*walks by tottering like a drunk, drowsily humming a song*)

COUNTRY GIRL: (*Appears in the clearing, carrying a package under her arm. She glances around fearfully. Then she takes a few steps forward again and looks back. Suddenly she jumps over to the anthill and tries to hide her package in it. She looks visibly distraught, her movements anxious. Finally she's able to hide her package. She backs away from the anthill and takes a few steps toward the woods. She looks around again,* *terrified. She tries to wipe the ants off her arms with quick movements. She stands still in one spot for a long time, staring blankly at the anthill.*)

FAT GENTLEMAN: (*returning*) You're still here. (*He sees his mistake.*) Oh, excuse me!

COUNTRY GIRL: (*lets out a feeble cry*)

FAT GENTLEMAN: Good evening, miss . . .

COUNTRY GIRL: Good evening . . .

FAT GENTLEMAN: Are you waiting for someone?

COUNTRY GIRL: I'm lost.

FAT GENTLEMAN: This path leads to the road. It's only twenty minutes by bus to the city.

COUNTRY GIRL: Thank you. (*She walks in the opposite direction.*)

FAT GENTLEMAN: Why are you running away from me?

COUNTRY GIRL: I'm not running away.

FAT GENTLEMAN: You have nothing to fear. I'm a respectable family man.

COUNTRY GIRL: (*starts to sob*)

FAT GENTLEMAN: (*approaching her*) Oh, please don't cry . . .

COUNTRY GIRL: Leave me alone.

FAT GENTLEMAN: I don't mean any harm.

COUNTRY GIRL: (*erupts in a fit of laughter*)

FAT GENTLEMAN: What's the matter with you?

COUNTRY GIRL: (*calming down*) Nothing, not a thing.

FAT GENTLEMAN: See? Not sulking suits you.

COUNTRY GIRL: You scared me.

FAT GENTLEMAN: Would you like some coffee?

COUNTRY GIRL: I'm parched.

FAT GENTLEMAN: (*pours her coffee*) It's excellent.

COUNTRY GIRL: (*drinks*) Thank you.

FAT GENTLEMAN: Anyway, we're going the same way, aren't we?

COUNTRY GIRL: Makes no difference to me where I go.

FAT GENTLEMAN: Not from around here?

COUNTRY GIRL: No, I don't know anyone here.

FAT GENTLEMAN: And in the city?

COUNTRY GIRL: I'm hoping to find a job there.

FAT GENTLEMAN: I see . . .

COUNTRY GIRL: I got no one.

FAT GENTLEMAN: There's ants all over the place. Let's go that way. Deeper into the woods.

COUNTRY GIRL: I ain't going nowhere with you.

FAT GENTLEMAN: I'll find you a job.

COUNTRY GIRL: No!

FAT GENTLEMAN: I'll make sure you're able to live in the city until things pick up for you.

COUNTRY GIRL: Not interested.

FAT GENTLEMAN: Here, take this, for the first few days.

COUNTRY GIRL: No, no, no . . .

FAT GENTLEMAN: I can't force you. But should you ever need any help . . . It's a pity that it's so late. My family is waiting for me at the edge of the woods. I just came back for my knife.

COUNTRY GIRL: Hear that? Mister, you hear that?

FAT GENTLEMAN: I don't hear a thing.

COUNTRY GIRL: You hear that crying?

FAT GENTLEMAN: You're right, as if someone were crying in the woods.

COUNTRY GIRL: In the woods? (*She laughs maniacally.*)

VOICE OF LITTLE GIRL: Mommy, mommy . . . (*Crying.*)

FAT GENTLEMAN: That's my daughter!

COUNTRY GIRL: Your daughter? (*She laughs maniacally.*)

FAT GENTLEMAN: My little girl . . .

COUNTRY GIRL: (*maniacally gestures at the anthill*) There, there, she's there.

VOICE OF CRYING LITTLE GIRL: (*coming from somewhere*)

COUNTRY GIRL: Give me back my child! (*She lunges at him.*)

FAT GENTLEMAN: I haven't done anything to you. Let go!

COUNTRY GIRL: Keep your promise!

FAT GENTLEMAN: I'll stab you if you don't stop choking me!

COUNTRY GIRL: (*grapples with him and yanks the knife from his hand*) And now you'll grovel on your knees. Kneel, or I'll kill you!

FAT GENTLEMAN: (*falling to his knees*) Help!

COUNTRY GIRL: Give me back my child you buried!

FAT GENTLEMAN: Help! A madwoman . . .

COUNTRY GIRL: (*points to the anthill*) Over there! Give her back to me! Give me back my little girl!

FAT GENTLEMAN: My children, my poor children, my poor wife!

COUNTRY GIRL: (*stabs him with the knife*) You dog, dig her up for me!

FAT GENTLEMAN: (*takes a few steps and drops to his knees in front of the anthill*)

COUNTRY GIRL: I ain't listening to no more of your promises. You disgust me, murderer. (*She stabs him again.*)

FAT GENTLEMAN: I'm innocent . . .

COUNTRY GIRL: (*stabs him again*) You showed me no mercy, why should I show you any? I'm a woman like any other. (*She stabs him three times.*)

FAT GENTLEMAN: (*staggers and falls onto the anthill, cries out, then lies motionless*)

COUNTRY GIRL: Revenge is sweet. I wrote you a thousand times, you never believed me. Suffer, suffer like you're in hell . . . (*She rifles through his pocket and finds a box of matches. She sets the anthill on fire. The flame blazes up and illuminates her. She throws the knife into the fire and runs into the woods. The fire spreads.*)

BOY: (*shouting in the distance*) Daddy, daddy . . .

ECHO: Daddy, daddy . . .

Curtain

4TH INTERLUDE

The front curtain rises. In front of the rear curtain stands a woodblock with a hatchet stuck in it. A rocking cradle is nearby. Slow, muffled drum beats.

Curtain

The Bird of Doom is good-hearted
Like children who peel oranges
But also those who burn the wings off flies
And spiders their America
The Bird of Doom is good-hearted
Like fire and its hunger
That doesn't prefer the raisins of a bundt cake
Over the down of useless linen cupboards
The Bird of Doom is good-hearted
Like a small alarm bell
Keeping you from sleep
Even when you're asleep even when you'd like to sleep
Many days and many nights
You will witness a great flood
Yet this pealing bell
Will not fall silent in a week or month or year
For there is nothing more terrible
Than a suffocating box
When that willful flail
Deals its final blow and has no strength for more

In a House of Mourning

A catafalque with the deceased. Dimly lit. Only candles illuminate the scene. Total silence.

WIDOWER: (*Lights the last candle. He heaves a great sigh. A knock on the door. He goes to the door and opens it. Whenever the door is opened, the sharp light of a bright day enters the mourning room. The* BIRD OF DOOM *now enters.*)

BIRD OF DOOM: (*silently gives his condolences to the* WIDOWER)

WIDOWER: Thank you. Thank you, sir. My late wife had great respect for you. Oh, those were the days, when you would play Beethoven together.

BIRD OF DOOM: Yes, those were beautiful times.

WIDOWER: Do you want to see her?

BIRD OF DOOM: I dare not ask.

WIDOWER: She hasn't changed a bit. (*He draws back the curtain.*)

BIRD OF DOOM: She's beautiful . . .

WIDOWER: It happened suddenly. We had just come back from a walk, she wanted me to fetch a book for her when she suddenly went pale, and before the doctor could do anything, her heart gave out. I cannot get my head around it, no, I simply cannot accept the fact that in a moment they will take her away . . . forever. Ah, my poor head . . .

BIRD OF DOOM: Is there anything I can do?

WIDOWER: Thank you. It would please me if you would help yourself to some refreshments in the next room. This way, please.

BIRD OF DOOM: Thank you. (*He walks to the door the* WIDOWER *opens.*)

WIDOWER: Forgive me for not going with you.

LADY FRIEND: (*Knocks and enters. The* WIDOWER *goes to greet her. Condolences.*)

WIDOWER: You were the first I told the terrible news.

LADY FRIEND: She often had premonitions of death. Not even a month back, she confided in me how anxiety would overwhelm her before falling asleep. She gave me this package and asked me to lay it at her feet in the coffin, and then she wanted her heart pierced with a knitting needle before the coffin was sealed shut.

WIDOWER: She never spoke of death with me.

LADY FRIEND: She did with me, quite often.

WIDOWER: I didn't realize she was keeping secrets from me.

LADY FRIEND: Every woman has her secrets.

WIDOWER: She didn't trust me?

LADY FRIEND: Why would you think that?

WIDOWER: It was you she entrusted with the package.

LADY FRIEND: Don't let it upset you.

WIDOWER: I was always as honest with her as a brother. She knew me better than I know myself. I assumed I knew her as well.

LADY FRIEND: She didn't confide everything, even to me.

WIDOWER: We lived a simple life.

LADY FRIEND: I never considered her simple.

WIDOWER: You're scaring me.

LADY FRIEND: Those marked for death never really completely trust us.

WIDOWER: (*in tears*) Marie, wake up, wake up . . . what are you keeping from me?

LADY FRIEND: Calm down.

WIDOWER: Oh, if only I had known . . .

LADY FRIEND: May I kiss her goodbye?

WIDOWER: She is so beautiful. Look. As though she were sleeping. (*He pulls back the curtain.*)

LADY FRIEND: Farewell, Marie, I'm returning your little secret. How many times have I wanted to know what you were keeping from me, but I never dared open the package. Goodbye . . . (*She begins to weep.*)

WIDOWER: Oh, how she's hurt me . . .

LADY FRIEND: (*places the package at the feet of the deceased*)

WIDOWER: I trusted her so much . . . Now I want to know her secret.

LADY FRIEND: You wouldn't dare to . . .

WIDOWER: I'll do as I like!

LADY FRIEND: You'd have the heart to?

WIDOWER: I want to be certain . . .

LADY FRIEND: What do you suspect her of?

WIDOWER: You are to blame.

LADY FRIEND: Poor Marie . . .

WIDOWER: I never suspected her of anything.

LADY FRIEND: I don't think there was any reason to.

WIDOWER: I'm opening the package.

LADY FRIEND: You shouldn't touch it, out of respect.

WIDOWER: Do you want me to go mad?

LADY FRIEND: Calm down, calm down . . .

WIDOWER: (*grabs the package*) My whole life is on the line . . .

LADY FRIEND: Please reconsider!

WIDOWER: No! (*He opens the package. A key falls out.*) A key . . . What does it mean?

LADY FRIEND: Really? Just a key?

WIDOWER: Just a key. (*He bends down for the key.*)

LADY FRIEND: It's rusty, look.

WIDOWER: I recognize it . . . It's the key to the garden of her parents' house. She gave it to me in secret so we could meet in the garden at night. That was so many years ago. And we even sold the house ten years back.

LADY FRIEND: But what does it mean?

WIDOWER: I don't know.

LADY FRIEND: Are you sure there's nothing else in the package?

WIDOWER: Yes. Wait a minute. A knitting needle.

LADY FRIEND: We've done her wrong.

WIDOWER: No, I was certain she wasn't keeping anything from me that would make me think less of her.

LADY FRIEND: But then what does the key mean?

WIDOWER: To me, her entire youth.

LADY FRIEND: And to her?

WIDOWER: In this circumstance? I don't know.

BIRD OF DOOM: (*knocks and enters*) I'm sorry. I was afraid you were alone.

WIDOWER: It's good you're here. You knew my wife, after all. Do you know why she wanted to be buried with this key? Surely she confided a few things to you when you would play Beethoven together.

BIRD OF DOOM: No, we hardly ever talked when we played.

WIDOWER: Excuse me, I didn't introduce you...

LADY FRIEND: (*shakes the* BIRD OF DOOM*'s hand*) We know each other. Once when she was sick, we played a Beethoven duet for her.

BIRD OF DOOM: I remember...

WIDOWER: I was sitting by her side then. How her eyes sparkled! She loved that piece more than anything. If it weren't crazy, I'd ask you to play it. As a farewell to her. But no, it's not crazy. Please play, play that piece.

BIRD OF DOOM: I'm afraid my hands are of no use today. And besides, it's never a good idea to dwell on what is gone forever.

WIDOWER: Please, I beg you. You'll ease my suffering. I'm sure of it.

BIRD OF DOOM: It will be very sad... (*He lets the* LADY FRIEND *go first as both exit through the door.*)

WIDOWER: (*He takes the key and wraps it up in the package, then takes it out again and examines it closely. The first notes of the music are heard.*) Marie, Marie, why this key, why did you keep secrets from me, wake up and tell me everything, Marie, you hear me? You hear? The key, why the key? Why didn't you trust me? Why must I resent you now? Wake up, Marie... (*He weeps.*)

UNDERTAKER: (*knocks and enters*) Excuse me, sir. I've come from the funeral parlor. It's time to nail the coffin shut.

WIDOWER: Wait in the foyer, sir. I'll call for you.

UNDERTAKER: Yes, of course... (*He exits.*)

WIDOWER: (*Sits at the table and holds his head in his hands. The* *music plays. Suddenly, the drapery stirs and the* DECEASED WIFE *slowly sits up in the coffin. She waves her hand.*)

DECEASED WIFE: Why all the candlelight?

WIDOWER: Marie! Marie!

DECEASED WIFE: I don't have a fever anymore. Ah, has he come?

WIDOWER: Marie, what does this key mean?

DECEASED WIFE: Key?

WIDOWER: Yes, the old key to the garden ...

DECEASED WIFE: Come back on Sunday. I'm tired ... Forgive me. I'm a woman like any other. (*She sinks back into the coffin.*)

WIDOWER: Speak, Marie. With whom did you have a tryst? Speak, or I'll stab your heart with the knitting needle. Was it him? The one who's playing piano? Admit it, was it him? Oh, how bitter I feel. Cursed key! Are you dead? Are you dead? Oh, yes, you certainly will be dead. (*He takes the needle and drives it through Marie's heart. Then he runs to the window, lifts up the curtain, stands motionless, then goes to the door, opens it, and motions with his hand.*)

UNDERTAKER: (*enters*)

WIDOWER: Nail the coffin shut. (*He exits to the room from where the music is coming.*)

UNDERTAKERS: (*carry in the coffin lid*)

Curtain

5TH INTERLUDE

The front curtain rises. Between the rear curtain and the apron is a white translucent screen where a shadow play is silhouetted: A naked woman treadles a sewing machine, which spins although it makes no sound. In her left hand the woman is holding a burning candle. A snuffer slowly approaches the candle, covers the candle's flame, and extinguishes it.

Curtain

The Bird of Doom is a friend to seafarers
And to all delicate creatures indifferent to life
Like a gunshot
Between two steep cliffs conversing
An indifferent dialogue
Between a man and a woman
Will become a dialogue between straw and flames
As soon as the cuckoo reckons the day
The straw will burn
The woman will leave
And the man will run off
Along a long thread that ends wherever
The Bird of Doom is a friend to seafarers
Like a lamp is an enemy to vagrants
He will leap dim the light stifle the scream
And long after him a void will remain

In a Passageway

A rather dark passageway. A stairway leads from the passageway on the left and right. It is raining. Several people with umbrellas enter the passageway. Wordlessly, they stand in a line. The men smoke.

TWENTY-YEAR-OLD WOMAN: (*Enters without an umbrella. She's soaked. She goes to stand in the line.*) Sir, what time is it?

CHAUFFEUR: 5:30.

TWENTY-YEAR-OLD WOMAN: Thank you.

BIRD OF DOOM: (*Enters, drenched, carrying a heavy suitcase. He places it on the ground and lights a cigar. It's evident he's worn out. He looks at the* CHAUFFEUR.) Sir, would you take this suitcase up to the fourth floor for me?

CHAUFFEUR: I'll gladly make an extra buck. (*He takes the suitcase.*) Left or right stairway?

BIRD OF DOOM: Fourth floor on the right, number seventeen.

CHAUFFEUR: As you wish. (*He carries off the suitcase. The* BIRD OF DOOM *follows him.*)

DAIRYMAID: This won't let up till evening.

TWENTY-YEAR-OLD WOMAN: You think so?

DAIRYMAID: Miss is drenched to the bone. It's not good for you.

TWENTY-YEAR-OLD WOMAN: What about taxis? They don't come here?

DAIRYMAID: Not usually.

TWENTY-YEAR-OLD WOMAN: Should I just risk the rain?

DAIRYMAID: A wisp of a girl like you? You'd melt in this downpour. Besides, your boyfriend will wait.

TWENTY-YEAR-OLD WOMAN: What makes you so certain I have a date?

DAIRYMAID: I can tell from how fidgety you are.

TWENTY-YEAR-OLD WOMAN: Well, the train waits for no one.

DAIRYMAID: Miss one, catch another . . .

TWENTY-YEAR-OLD WOMAN: Easy for you to say.

CHAUFFEUR: (*returns*)

TWENTY-YEAR-OLD WOMAN: If only I could phone from someplace.

CHAUFFEUR: There's a telephone on the fourth floor. In that man's apartment. Right in the foyer.

TWENTY-YEAR-OLD WOMAN: You think I could impose on him?

CHAUFFEUR: He got just as drenched as you.

TWENTY-YEAR-OLD WOMAN: Which door is it?

CHAUFFEUR: Seventeen.

TWENTY-YEAR-OLD WOMAN: Thank you. (*She leaves toward the stairs.*)

DAIRYMAID: Took a lot out of you, eh?

CHAUFFEUR: Me? What about him?

DAIRYMAID: In such a downpour.

CHAUFFEUR: They're all nuts.

DAIRYMAID: Some bookworm?

CHAUFFEUR: Not books, no, those wouldn't make me sweat like a pig.

DAIRYMAID: Wouldn't be too sure about that . . .

CHAUFFEUR: He was carrying stones.

DAIRYMAID: No way!

CHAUFFEUR: A scholar or something.

DAIRYMAID: The things folks get up to for fun.

CHAUFFEUR: I guess it pays off.

DAIRYMAID: Maybe he's a gem collector.

CHAUFFEUR: It just keeps coming down.

DAIRYMAID: My milk will go sour and I'll lose money.

CHAUFFEUR: My boss will chew me out for not being at my post.

DAIRYMAID: Rain like this can cause a lot of trouble.

CHAUFFEUR: Damn weather . . .

DAIRYMAID: You can't complain. People take taxis when it rains.

CHAUFFEUR: Oh, but the skidding!

DAIRYMAID: I think I'll be going.

CHAUFFEUR: Not that you want to.

DAIRYMAID: I'm getting cold.

CHAUFFEUR: Want me to warm you up?

DAIRYMAID: Ugh!

CHAUFFEUR: If my old lady could hear me, I wouldn't be allowed home. (*He laughs.*)

DAIRYMAID: And she'd be right, too. (*Shouts can be heard coming from the stairway.*) Did you hear that?

CHAUFFEUR: Like someone's calling for help. (*More shouts on the stairway.*)

DAIRYMAID: It's a woman's voice.

CHAUFFEUR: Some hysteric.

DAIRYMAID: What a ruckus they're making up there . . .

TWENTY-YEAR-OLD WOMAN: (*runs out naked from the stairway, shouting, and rushes into the passageway*)

DAIRYMAID: Christ almighty!

TWENTY-YEAR-OLD WOMAN: Help, help! (*She dashes out of the passageway into the rain.*)

CHAUFFEUR: (*goggle-eyed at the fleeing* TWENTY-YEAR-OLD WOMAN)

DAIRYMAID: Why, it's that young lady . . .

CHAUFFEUR: (*stares into the rain*)

DAIRYMAID: Cat got your tongue? What a hussy . . .

CHAUFFEUR: Who was that?

DAIRYMAID: It's clear what you were gawking at if you didn't recognize her.

CHAUFFEUR: It happened so suddenly, like a bolt of lightning . . .

DAIRYMAID: You've turned into a pillar of salt!

CHAUFFEUR: Who was it?

DAIRYMAID: That lady who went up to use the telephone.

CHAUFFEUR: To the fourth floor?

DAIRYMAID: Some scholar!

CHAUFFEUR: You think he wanted to lock her in there?

DAIRYMAID: I'm calling the police on him.

CHAUFFEUR: He didn't look the type.

DAIRYMAID: What will she do naked on the street, in the rain?

CHAUFFEUR: She'll get arrested.

DAIRYMAID: The cops are holed up indoors.

CHAUFFEUR: I should lend her my coat . . .

DAIRYMAID: We know all about that . . .

CHAUFFEUR: I should at least go up to the fourth floor and find out what happened.

DAIRYMAID: What if she's lost her mind?

CHAUFFEUR: It was a little nuts.

DAIRYMAID: She was definitely on her way to see someone off. I gathered that from what she said. We should take a closer look at this scholar of ours.

CHAUFFEUR: Why would she take her clothes off? I mean, it's silly, why does a woman take her clothes off . . .

DAIRYMAID: I know what must've happened. He must've told her to dry out her clothes, and then . . .

CHAUFFEUR: I'll go find out . . . (*He runs toward the stairway.*)

DAIRYMAID: Careful, be careful . . .

TWENTY-YEAR-OLD MAN: (*completely drenched, he peers into the passageway*) Anežka, are you here?

DAIRYMAID: Hello, who are you looking for?

TWENTY-YEAR-OLD MAN: (*steps into the passageway and shakes out his hat, water dripping from it*)

DAIRYMAID: Watch out, don't knock over my milk can.

TWENTY-YEAR-OLD MAN: Sorry . . . Have you been here long?

DAIRYMAID: Why? Looking for someone?

TWENTY-YEAR-OLD MAN: My girlfriend. She called to tell me she was taking cover from the rain around here somewhere.

DAIRYMAID: And how did you get here from the station so quickly?

TWENTY-YEAR-OLD MAN: I took a taxi to the corner of the street. But who told you I was at the station?

DAIRYMAID: She did.

TWENTY-YEAR-OLD MAN: I checked in all the passageways and not a soul anywhere. Where is she?

DAIRYMAID: Ah, how should I put this . . .

TWENTY-YEAR-OLD MAN: Just give it to me straight.

DAIRYMAID: I think something's happened to her . . .

TWENTY-YEAR-OLD MAN: Oh Christ, in her pocketbook, she had . . .

DAIRYMAID: What?

TWENTY-YEAR-OLD MAN: Where is she? Where is she? Tell me everything.

CHAUFFEUR: (*He runs out from the stairwell, in his hands a woman's dress on fire. The scene is lit.*) Poor girl. It burned right off of her.

TWENTY-YEAR-OLD MAN: My God, those are her clothes! Anežka, Anežka, we could've died so beautifully, why did I ever let you leave? A woman like any other.

DAIRYMAID: (*splashes milk on the burning dress*) How could this have happened?

TWENTY-YEAR-OLD MAN: I curse a world where love is an evil! (*He shoots himself and falls to the ground.*)

CHAUFFEUR: Damn this blasted weather . . .

Curtain

The front curtain rises. Three barber chairs stand in front of the rear curtain. Three men sit in them, their heads wrapped in white cloths, which form a kind of knot. This shadow play is cast on the translucent screen between the rear curtain and the apron: A woman completely nude save a blindfold over her eyes is sharpening a straight razor. Each of the men, their backs turned to the audience, holds a mirror. At fixed intervals the mirrors fall from their hands and shatter.

Curtain

The Bird of Doom does not know his name
Like the cabbage rose
And like you do not know in a dream
The actions that triggered it
The Bird of Doom does not know his homeland
Like a snake on the neck of a woman
Who flaunts it
Like flowerbeds their childish handwriting
The Bird of Doom does not know his victims
Like a moneybag does not know its weight
Like pleasure does not know the despair it's created
Like rope does not know its end
Though if he did know
He would be even crueler
Than man himself
Whom he moves like a puppet
Because nothing is more beautiful
Than to forget about pain
When feeling even deeper pain
Like fire in the fireplace
And so the Bird of Doom
Roasts in his own cinders
To be golden as the morning star
That sears eternity

In Front of a Stand

In front of a stand selling peanuts. On the corner of two smaller streets in the city center.

OWNER: Peanuts!

PEDESTRIAN: One cone.

OWNER: (*hands over the cone*) Thank you kindly.

PEDESTRIAN: Ten cigarettes.

OWNER: I don't sell cigarettes. (*Takes out his cigarette case.*) May I offer you one?

PEDESTRIAN: Thank you. (*He exits.*)

OWNER: Peanuts!

ANOTHER PEDESTRIAN: (*walks past*)

OWNER: Peanuts!

CHAMBERMAID: (*walking past, elegantly dressed*)

OWNER: Peanuts! A cone for you, ma'am?

CHAMBERMAID: (*stops in front of the stand, looks in wonder at the* OWNER) Is that you, boss . . . ?

OWNER: How are you doing, miss?

CHAMBERMAID: Fine, thank you. Knock on wood.

NEW PEDESTRIAN: (*walks past*)

OWNER: Peanuts!

CHAMBERMAID: I can't believe my eyes.

OWNER: That other business didn't work out.

CHAMBERMAID: To this day I don't know what that club was really all about.

OWNER: An experiment. A vile experiment . . . And how are you?

CHAMBERMAID: I'm happy.

OWNER: Happy people do still exist in the world then.

CHAMBERMAID: Well, I value my . . . oh, I better not repeat the word. You never know . . .

OWNER: You look great, like you just walked off a catwalk.

CHAMBERMAID: You're just saying that . . . I'm happy with my life, and so people think that . . . Anyway, you take care.

OWNER: I'm hoping it'll pick up. (*He hands her a business card.*) Stop by if you're ever bored . . .

CHAMBERMAID: (*looks at the card*) The Optimists' Club. What's that?

OWNER: A new experiment.

CHAMBERMAID: Sounds more cheerful.

OWNER: The clientele won't be packing revolvers.

CHAMBERMAID: Good luck. (*She exits.*)

OWNER: Peanuts!

BIRD OF DOOM: (*rises up on a corner and pastes posters on a wall*)

SCHOOLGIRL: (*walking past*)

OWNER: Peanuts! Buy some, little lady, buy two, get one free.

SCHOOLGIRL: (*stops and looks at the cones*)

OWNER: Care to buy some, little lady?

SCHOOLGIRL: How much for a cone?

OWNER: Half a crown for the little lady.

SCHOOLGIRL: And if I buy two, I get one free?

OWNER: Just for you.

SCHOOLGIRL: Hope you're not gypping yourself, mister . . .

OWNER: Why in such a hurry, little lady?

SCHOOLGIRL: I'm going to look at the posters to see what's playing at the children's theater.

OWNER: I know a children's theater where you could perform.

SCHOOLGIRL: They wouldn't take me.

OWNER: And if I say they would?

SCHOOLGIRL: What role would I be playing?

OWNER: We'll see.

SCHOOLGIRL: I'd have to ask my mom first.

OWNER: Better to surprise mommy.

SCHOOLGIRL: She'd be mad at me.

OWNER: They're looking for a girl just like you.

SCHOOLGIRL: Really?

OWNER: How old are you?

SCHOOLGIRL: Thirteen.

OWNER: Excellent. That's perfect.

SCHOOLGIRL: Where is the theater?

OWNER: Just a little ways from here. I'll take you there.

SCHOOLGIRL: But someone'll steal all your peanuts.

OWNER: That man over there will keep an eye on them.

SCHOOLGIRL: Here's a crown for the nuts.

OWNER: Keep it.

SCHOOLGIRL: How can you make ends meet?

OWNER: It's just two cones . . .

SCHOOLGIRL: (*returns the cones*) I can't accept them for free. Mom would get mad at me.

OWNER: What does your daddy do?

SCHOOLGIRL: He died.

OWNER: And mommy?

SCHOOLGIRL: She's a seamstress.

OWNER: If you performed in the theater, you could help your mommy earn a little extra.

SCHOOLGIRL: Mom wouldn't allow it, she says children shouldn't have to earn money.

OWNER: Shall we go?

SCHOOLGIRL: No, another time. I'll ask Mom for permission.

OWNER: It looks like you've got a cavity. You should get it fixed. A girl has to have nice teeth to appear on stage.

SCHOOLGIRL: I don't have any cavities.

OWNER: Then I was mistaken? Could you show me?

SCHOOLGIRL: (*opens her mouth a bit*)

OWNER: (*stuffs a gag into her mouth*) A woman like any other.

BIRD OF DOOM: (*rushes up and lightning quick pulls out rope and binds the* SCHOOLGIRL's *legs*)

OWNER: (*binding her hands*) The car's around the corner.

BIRD OF DOOM: (*grabs the struggling girl and carries her offstage*)

OWNER: Peanuts! (*He starts packing up his stand.*)

MIDDLE-AGED MAN: (*walks past*)

OWNER: Peanuts! Buy some, sir . . .

MIDDLE-AGED MAN: Got a light?

OWNER: Here you are, sir. (*He lights his cigarette.*)

MIDDLE-AGED MAN: Thank you. Now, to be polite, I should buy a cone in exchange, but I have to confess, I don't care for peanuts.

OWNER: Truth be told, I don't either. But if the gentleman would like, I could offer something more pleasing. (*He reaches into his pocket for a picture postcard.*) Take a look.

MIDDLE-AGED MAN: Hmm, nudie postcards? I've seen my share, but I'm not a collector.

OWNER: The gentleman must prefer the real thing.

MIDDLE-AGED MAN: It's no more interesting.

OWNER: On this point I disagree with the gentleman. I mean, if you're thinking about wine bars and all those lounges, sure, but there are also legitimate private establishments that offer genuine entertainment, where real fun can be had.

MIDDLE-AGED MAN: Don't be so sure.

OWNER: If the gentleman desires, I will prove it to him.

MIDDLE-AGED MAN: When you open a newspaper and read any of those silly ads feigning an air of mystery it turns you off straightaway.

OWNER: Genuine entertainment establishments that offer something unique do not advertise. If the gentleman is discreet, however, and is interested in something truly spectacular, I can share this business card.

MIDDLE-AGED MAN: The Optimists' Club? Doesn't ring a bell.

OWNER: Even so, nowhere else might you meet such young women without fear of being disturbed.

MIDDLE-AGED MAN: I'm not that old yet.

OWNER: If the gentleman is ever bored, he has the address. It was in no way my intention to trouble him.

MIDDLE-AGED MAN: Actually, I'll have one of those cones after all.

OWNER: Here you are. (*He hands the man a cone.*) Thank you kindly.

MIDDLE-AGED MAN: Goodbye.

OWNER: My regards, sir. (*He starts packing up his stand.*) Peanuts!

CHAMBERMAID: (*enters the scene holding the hand of the* SCHOOL-GIRL, *who is bawling uncontrollably*)

SCHOOLGIRL: (*stops crying and points at the* OWNER) That's him. (*She starts crying, pulls away from the* CHAMBERMAID, *and runs off.*)

CHAMBERMAID: Do you know what's in store for you?

OWNER: May I help you?

CHAMBERMAID: Do you know what's in store for you? Ah, now it all finally makes sense. (*She pulls out the business card from her bag and flings it at the* OWNER's *feet.*) I'm ashamed to even know you!

OWNER: It's never good to know too much. (*He picks up the business card. Then he rushes at the* CHAMBERMAID *and begins to choke her.*)

CHAMBERMAID: (*falls lifelessly to the ground*)

OWNER: Too much happiness never pays off. (*He darts over to his cart and quickly wheels it offstage.*) Peanuts . . .

Curtain

Brief Epilogue

The front curtain rises. A wardrobe stands in front of the rear curtain. A YOUNG LAD enters the scene, dressed in a knight's costume from a play. He is holding a book in his left hand, silently memorizing text, clearly alexandrines, and a rapier in his right hand, which emphasizes his silent declamations. Suddenly, the door of the wardrobe partly opens. The YOUNG LAD fixes his gaze on it, pauses, throws down his book, and in two or three leaps is at the wardrobe. A sack falls out of the wardrobe. The YOUNG LAD sinks his rapier into it, whereupon red liquid gushes out. The YOUNG LAD stares speechless at the bleeding sack.

YOUNG LAD: (*to himself*) I have slain the Bird of Doom . . .

Curtain

5

MANUSCRIPT OF AN EVENING

1.

You play the ace
And someone steps in your path
Bordered
Like oakwood by a thunderstorm

A bay window
The door opens and someone enters
To toss a spark
You don't know why is ablaze

A tiny snail
Crawls to a spot
Where a statue is sensitive
As the instinct of a sunflower

And a sore mark
Left by a flute
The broken chandelier of evening
Cloaks in darkness

2.

One day a shepherd sang
And no one knew where
When he sang a procession marched
When he did not it rained

One day his singing stopped
And again the procession marched
While it also rained
And the twilight was immense

Two processions marched in darkness
One downhill and one uphill
They never knew they passed on the way
They were blind they were blind

There is a haystack I adore
When it burns up I will forget
Who I was
And the light will be immense

3.

The beautiful month of July
The wind like a sleepwalker grazes
Red girls who quiver
And wild circles on the pond

A dragonfly plaintively whirls
Its futile flight
Like you who hovers
In a box without wings

The art of hanging by a thread
By no means fearless and yet
The tree frog calls to Her Majesty the Moon
Three lightning flashes and a horse in a desolate landscape

4.

As agreed
The person of black entered
When the woman of white exited

5.

My head heavy
From gardens I've never walked
A nightmare oppresses me
Because I cannot find you

You redhead
With eyes like wind
To whom I could say
It is the end of days

The end of weariness the end of searching
The end of all histories so precious
Better that I end this clairvoyant text
Someone has dictated to me

6

SURREALIST EXPERIMENTATION

WHY I AM A SURREALIST
An Irrational Definition

I am a surrealist
    For the shrieks of dreams
    For the shrieks of dreams to open the torture chamber door
                                    to human mystery
    For the shrieks of dreams for the key to childhood
    For the keyhole of night
    For my hatred of the mirror
    For my head busted against a headboard
    For ghosts in a sack
    For the flour chest and engravings in dime novels
    For the closed book on a high shelf
    For the price lists of orthopedic products
    For the mystery of the holes in a rattan chair
    For the rustle in the chimney
    For the indigestion from the Eucharist
    For the confessor's bad breath
    For the joy of targeting a cop's nose
    For Thursday on Sunday
    For the sauerkraut of barrack walls
    For the hatred of romantic gibberish
    For the tedium of lies
    For the ridiculousness of egoism
    For indifference to death
    For the futility of travel
    For the clairvoyance of friendship
    For the sun with its crown of night that is André Breton

For the morning star that is Paul Éluard
For the telescope and microscope of his poetry
For the burning resinous wreaths of Benjamin Péret's imagery
For the Columbian eggs of Max Ernst's collages
For Man Ray's seismograph
For the otherworldly plant messages in the paintings
of Yves Tanguy
For the topsy-turvy Inquisition that is Salvador Dalí
For the support in the eyes of all other Surrealists
For the long nights of my Prague friends
For a classless society
For the beauty that "will be convulsive or will not be at all"

A SURREALIST GAME

— *If I were not a sick woman*
— *The hand would hold special significance in a chess match*

— *If you were not afraid*
— *Corks would float on water*

— *If people were different*
— *The city would resemble a cat*

— *If it were not raining*
— *I would go looking for bamboo*

— *If there were no school*
— *Wind would twirl to the music of a street organ*

— *If you were not a poet*
— *All the windows would be fake*

— *If I as a woman wanted to write*
— *Blue dye would run in brooks*

●

— *When children think hard before speaking*
— *I will leave*

— *When mustaches are made of fire*
— *We will enlarge photographs*

— When leaves no longer fall from trees
— We will no longer know each other

— When the chimney sweep stops under the window
— School will begin

— When thunder booms
— I will go to sleep

— When work becomes a pointless luxury
— Many people will perish

— When she rings your doorbell
— We will roast her

— When a drum utters the word no
— Justice will reign

●

— The more women resemble luminous willows
— The more we will fight back

— The more the flame blackens
— The more the number of wretched

— The more haystacks that burn
— The more I will love him

— The more a good word holds true
— The more muck there will be

— *The more letters the mailman loses*
— *The more he will earn*

— *The more statues destroyed by hail*
— *The more they will laugh*

— *The more women who die*
— *The more I will get*

●

— *If you leave me*
— *The branch will leaf*

— *If they occupy the region*
— *Grasshoppers will celebrate*

— *If justice reigns*
— *Peas will bombard a peaceful village*

— *If you are brave*
— *Canvas will grow on trees*

— *If we have little money*
— *The wheels will spin aimlessly*

— *If your health improves*
— *A gun barrel will scare no one*

— *If you call into the woods*
— *The thrush will be king of the birds*

— *If you get a job*
— *A bell will ring in the woods*

— *If you demand it*
— *18 teeth will be black and 18 white*

The halberd of a soft wood sorrel would be more inclined to a fly than to a patron of canvas. The earl banished the nightingale from an olive sash and reveres rifles. Three pitiful white partridges are a rarer sight here on the nettle film of a winter valley of pelicans than an imp in a festive cask. The stick snapped as soon as the tiger came within range. I don't know what name the shrike took but thunder echoed for a whole hour across the ants' raion. The curse is coming true. The happy mutt watches over Liza and the stuttering child has dashed off into the woods. I like vanilla just as much as cilantro. Both thrill me. The harsher the winter the more mesmerizing the swaddling that litter the colorful meadows. Let us make our living by guillotining birds as some crones make a living from ornithomancy. The crazy bridge can't catch up to the violin wailing in the cracked willow. The stable is readied for the king of turkeys and the bells ring. As far as the eye can see, juniper is burning everywhere. Never again will I walk out gloveless during that black April with its machine burned to the wick. If the battle lasted another hour the kind curls would no longer be owned by a dreamy paracelsus who got his name from a device for measuring humidity. Grass snakes in their holes tackle milt a certain bandit has fabricated. Six cards and the seventh a monk. We shall finally begin our march against heads in electrically charged capacitor plates. Salt preserved our happy arrival on this miraculous globe. I'm angry. Three times now I've called to no avail the old herbwoman who vanishes with her cape. A merry and happy New Year.

7

PONT DU CARROUSEL

THE FIGHT FOR THE SEEING MAN

What is a man to make of himself amid endless angst
And what could he be
If despicable speculation did not tear the bread from his lips
He works eats and ages
Like his teeth
Hunched over his machine
He thinks of his family
Closes his eyes in dread of the future
Embittered he begets children
And dies before his time
How could such a man see
Until he's totally insane
How could he have insight into his imagination
Sheepishly he shoos a dream from his wrinkled brow
Hitting rock bottom he reaches for the bottle
In ignorance of himself he commits crimes
His odious subjugators have it no better
All their time is dedicated to breaking him
And to fretting over their gold
Their criminality betrays a complete lack of imagination
They fear assassinations
And act as if one foot's in the grave
How could a poet possibly have a place in this society
So sometimes he understands madhouse inmates
At his most human he seems an outright lunatic
Not made to put up a fight
What a colossal mistake

Wanting to wheedle maxims out of him
That might serve the public good
Until a joie de vivre itself is this good
Joy for life's invisible aspects
Which must be made visible
But won't be on a wider scale
Until human prehistory has its reckoning
I had to say it
But now be gone prosaic thought
Time flies and a poem is rapping at my door

PONT DU CARROUSEL

The arms of rivers and the arms of women embrace in a dance
The summer night a thousand-year-old brood hen flies
                                    the astral coop and cackles
The Rhine gold of vineyards ripens
And a hundred-headed performer rides into towns
He's an old potter
He pipes on his ocarina a melody composed by a gale
A horde of children in tow
And a waddling gaggle of women welcomes him
Sheathed in straw like his pots
His blind eyes crush tears like lice
That make his face an anthill
Yet he has one more eye in the bluish bump on his forehead
A prescient eye
And new retinues arrive
A man with alligator skin
A barren woman who's returned from Lourdes
A child kangaroo
Conjoined twins
A lunatic who covers his head with manure
They keep arriving with others mumbling an unintelligible prayer

The potter goes on piping his song
A song that has forded many rivers
A song sung by a Dutch fisherman
And the sick get on a rickety carousel

Sleep is so beautiful
Its blindness sees farther than your watchful eyes
Coming to a standstill on the steps of night
Where a legendary snake writhes

I have slept everywhere
Mostly on bridges
Where rivers weave memory
Everywhere and mostly on long walks
A rose touched me with its bell
On the threshold of Herculaneum
Where I came upon women with no knowledge of the sun
Women in coffins drawn by a swan
I have slept like a rock in the middle of roads
I have slept away long Sundays over the lichen of walls
Many a time cornflower has lulled me to sleep
Today I sleep whenever I remember his clay flute

Old women kneel in prayer on the miraculous carousel
And rain assails cities
Changing them into harpists
The old women mutter their rosaries
Then suddenly feel like something bit them
A magical watch ticks under the barren woman's heart
Seventy-year-old women dance a jig
The lunatic no longer sticks out his tongue at swarms of flies

Such a beautiful day oh how you would forget it
We walked alongside the festive lanterns of the illuminated Vltava
You stayed silent as I wept

Like night turned into a skyrocket
Do you still remember that small smiling blind man
Who said the word offspring
You were trembling like the voice of the street organ
Lamenting like my youth like myself
We walked from bridge to bridge
Pressed together as if on a carousel
Afraid of saying goodbye
Afraid of sleep afraid of words
Then we went into a wine bar near your place
A few gloomy women sitting there
Your green eyes wandered over the wallpaper
We drank bad sweetish wine I can still taste it to this day
Why does that night appear to me as an ocarina
Gifted to me once by a potter in exchange for a knot of rags
Why am I no longer moved by the protestations you often cry
Why are wine bars so dreary why is it so hard for me to fall asleep
The performer disappeared and with him that extravagant entourage
Of all the things I've loved only my urban wanderlust remains
I pursue unfathomable adventures
Like the hundred-headed potter
He has a cage with a single mouse
And he pipes on his ocarina
A ditty he never thinks about
And so he goes from town to town like the chorus of his song
He is a great hypnotizer older than his companion the moon
He is a great friend to lovers
From the day I met him I often gaze into the unknown
Into the unknown from which sweet and frightening beings

come to me

The arms of rivers and the arms of women embrace in a dance
The summer night a thousand-year-old brood hen flies
$$\text{the astral coop and cackles}$$
The Rhine gold of vineyards ripens
Today I dream of finally seeing Lorelei!

THE TRAPDOOR

I greet your gliding flight O wings of death
But there are other signs too

I went walking with my girlfriend last night
In a marshy landscape
Which is what I call a few freshly plowed fields
Just outside the city
It was swampland once
The sky on certain days is also swamp
Autumn was on its way

We walked like that for an hour
And it was as beautiful as forgetting
The world and your own self
As beautiful as forgetting that you were alive
And I felt terrible like a drowned man being resuscitated
When my girlfriend spoke
I felt terrible like a drowned man who'd forgotten he had ever lived

Luckily her words were vague
She said
I feel sad
And then
How terrible the roads that end in fields
And also
I dread distant lights
Those uncertain and distant graveyard lights

And then
How sad it is to look into windows where people are eating dinner

I owed her a reply
Like a wet leaf owes a spark
Like a trumpet owes the evening
Like a cobwebbed mirror owes a candle
Like withering wax owes a ring
I owed her a reply and so we now walked in silence

Suddenly I felt
But just for a moment
That the earth had spun away from its orbit and was falling
I was falling along with the entire landscape
I was falling
Still walking on firm ground
I was falling feeling vertigo
That was not vertigo
I was falling like a tower that sees its birds take flight
I was falling like a man whose memory leaves him
I was falling with no pain
I was falling like the cindery fall of a glowing cigar
I was falling like a burning sheet of paper that consumes a poem
I was falling like a swingboat
I was falling like a drop into snow
Like a bell into a lake
Like a child into an eiderdown
Like a nut on a bolt
I was falling feeling no impact
I was falling with the entire landscape with its invisible swamp

I was falling but it was just a feeling of forgetting
Reality faded quietly dissipating
Like July on a rooster's head
Like the resin of a dying star
Like a midnight fly
Like a telegram in a forest
Like a China of November snowdrifts
Like the smile of dew at noon
I was falling like Earth falls in its flight through space

I greet your gliding flight O wings of death
Those who resisted it
Have purple faces
Have bloodshot eyes like a withering grape leaf
Have terrible scars on their brow
Have fingernails digging into their palm lines
Have hair standing on end
Have a wooden tongue and petrified limbs
O let me put myself into her hands
Like the ailing to narcosis
Like the wounded to a surgeon's scalpel
Like weary eyes to sleep
Like a woman's womb to hot semen
Like my hands to my thoughts
Adrift like mutable clouds over the chaotic land

THE ELEMENTS

Old man on earth woman in water man in fire child in air
That history inconstant as Proteus

Clods of earth like calloused palms
An old peasant plantation fighter
Breaks the wind into fence posts
Old peasant dung beetle
Extracts sapphires in a hard-coal basin
Like the roots of teeth
He carries in his pouch mountains broken into shards
His brow is a mill
This champion of labor breaks rocks with his heart
He is a merciless colossus
His fingers are twisted roots
His phallus is the phallus of a thresher
His thoughts collide with his house
And shake its foundations
Brutal as a cannon
His chest hirsute with thistle
He abhors gentleness
When he sleeps boulder rubble rolls down the hillside
When he sleeps snaking rivers ultimately gush from his temples
Let's give the floor for a moment to his daughters
On whom he forced bones
But that's also all he did
They conceal this hereditary sign as best they can
They stretch spinelessly in the velvet of a reeded streambed

Their fingers repeating an eternal trill
Their tongue present wherever water leaks through
Their tongue rough as a honeycomb
Remember the Erinyes of rainfalls
They would kiss you to death if they could
In the morning after a horrific dream you find their fleeting kisses
                                                    on your brow

Sometimes they are crowned queen by a rainbow
You can taste them even in your saliva
O river coiling in a mirabelle
My poems profess your waltzing litheness
River dancing on tiptoes
Cold you feign fire
My most intrinsic element

When the skeletons of two rivers rub against each other a fire ignites
Let us chase the marathon runner torchbearer
Hiding in a field menacingly brandishing a red poppy
Wherever he's stepped heather is branded into the earth
He spits like a volcano into the crowns of apple trees
At the touch of the crest of his hair you burn O starry night
His leg is a lightning bolt
He hops as if on a cimbalom
And drives turkeys crazy
He has scorched the underbelly of a kingfisher
And scatters carrion beetles between the fields like a pyromaniac
His red eyes peek out from cherry leaves
Spring blushes when recalling his fireworks
At dawn and dusk he enters rivers
Like Narcissus his reflection

I listen to the buzz of a fly
And watch how air is born
Taut on the highest string
Memory itself
A cloud
A phantom disgorged by horses' nostrils
A piper with bagpipes like lungs slung over his shoulder
Evening hovering
With a child's tears
That curdle into porridge
Driven by the wind into my mouth
Only to have a sigh escape it
Like a slumbering bee
Like those iridescent bubbles bursting in the infinite distance

In the end our life is nothing but an interplay of the elements
Our life our death
Our love our misfortune our endlessly changing history

HEAT LIGHTNING

Something effervescent is in your morning thought
The more memory moves away from oblivion
Like the earth from clouds
The more suddenly lightning is about to join them with
                                        a fire-flash kiss

I adored nights of heat lightning
Starless nights when the sky resembled a glassworks
I observe its mirrored signals
But there's another heat lightning too

I slowly forget the gum tree
That is woman
Miraculously multiplying in the changing rooms of swimming pools
For the locker with her dress seems to me much more nostalgic
I crave its phantom
In a dead-end street
Heartless myself once more I anticipate your lost gaze
Woman with eyes of jasmine
I can still taste sleep on the lips
For I have drunk too deep from the bottle of mystery

Let others invoke a sober life
I will keep following in the footsteps of the sleepwalker
I have been and who we were
Before your eyes lost their power over me
I hate the kisses of insatiable egoists

I hate the kisses with which a woman lures a man to the altar
As I hate sentimentality
For I have kissed a Siren's lips
O mad love
I have come to know your opium dens
That is why I'm a stranger on the carousel of collective courting
In a copse with the brief blazes of matches

Once there was a blind man as beautiful as a garnet rose
Who loved evenings
When everywhere grew dark
As in his mind
He went for walks through the most beautiful gardens in the world
Sometimes he would doff his hat in greeting
One day he became acquainted with a woman by her scent
She was as beautiful as he had always hoped
Together they went for walks every day
He couldn't see her and she didn't know since she was blind herself
Their drowned bodies were found near the rowboat they took on
                                        a swollen river
This is not an allegory
And the city's bells toll loudly
It's getting dark
I hear in the distance a plaintive trumpeting
Every courtyard trembles with the song
Prolonging its tremolo forever
It's evening
One of the most humid yet and summer soon setting sail
Like the Grand Vizier in the *Arabian Nights*
Four trumpeters have ascended the battlements

And one by one sink beneath the length of the song
Stealing into every locked room
The clock chimes
And love comes out to hunt with an electric comb
It is a cricket with a kaleidoscopic globe head
It is anxiety in the form of a bridge with snakes for legs
It is the phrase *I love* in a fierce struggle with a bat
It is the ending of a bird's good-night call
It is the flute of the smallest windows
It is the gaze a cat's yowl throws at me
It is the magnesium of an approaching storm
Flooding all the city squares with foreboding
O heat lighting

Women stroll past a heavy cloud shrouding their desire
I walk by their laughter
And close my eyes to avoid going blind
On the promenade of sparklers
They are most beautiful when walking away
Around the corner where there are three times as many
So I feel
As if I'm adrift on a ship with burning sails

MERLIN

Merlin lives in old hollow statues
He has grown fond of a few desolate city squares
He loves Prague
I caught a glimpse of him once at the Knights of the Cross

                                              monastery

His head's covered in rust
He has the eyes of a wild cat
And a pointy mustache
He only sees in the dark
The remains of swallow nests cover his head
He gnaws old rotting beams with excellent teeth
In houses on the brink of collapse
He likes to roam libraries at night
And read everything ever written about him
His dirty fingernails scribble question marks in the margins

                                     of his mythical histories

He also likes museums
Concealed in armor he observes the people of the twentieth century
Having no desire to partake in life himself
He is a majestic observer and immensely amused
Sometimes overcome with nausea
Here he takes refuge in underground tunnels
He knows since he was there when they were built
There he curls into a ball and weeps softly
Though he believes in his power
That guarantees him eternal life
He often sleeps for years

And deeply regrets having slept through the Great War
People with imagination interest him
Sometimes he reveals himself to them
I met him under unusual circumstances
Once when a certain woman
Had me on the brink of despair
I loved her though she was married
We often walked through nighttime Prague
And met in hidden lanes
We stayed in the most dismal hotels
One day she had to hastily go abroad
And had no time to tell me
I walked around the Knights of the Cross
Where we were supposed to meet
And when she didn't show I decided to end my miserable existence
Just then I spotted Merlin
His eyes aglitter
Yet his gaze was very kind
And he beckoned me to follow him
Leading me through Prague's back streets
Wordlessly showing me several magical squares
I was spellbound
And when he disappeared I was certain I would go on living
Living for the beauty of things that seem of little worth
For the peculiar mystery of certain streets
To my surprise I spotted him this year in Paris
I was staying at Place du Panthéon
At that magical square resembling its namesake
My friend fell seriously ill and was taken to the hospital
I had the room to myself

I looked out my window at night whenever the Panthéon

                                                    clock chimed

One time I was returning very late
I didn't feel like sleeping
I was sad
And looked at the empty square
I then realized the Panthéon is a tomb
I realized this for the first time then
I was walking for a long time
Doubting everything I had ever loved
On the steps sat an old man
I thought he was sleeping
It was Merlin
He motioned for me to sit with him
He spoke impeccable French
I didn't understand everything he said
Nothing enamored him more than observing humankind's progress
He wondered how the world would change in a hundred years
Once a century he falls in love
He'd attended the funerals of several of his lovers
He'd also wanted to commit suicide
For that is the only way he could leave this world
He always recovered from his grief
And he goes on living
It's beautiful to live he said even as a blind man
Even without legs
Even in poverty
Even with a terrible illness
He smiled
All at once I saw his phallus sticking up

As he gaped wide-eyed at a passing car
With a woman sitting inside
Whom he said would be his first love of the twentieth century
He tore the swallow's nest from his brow
And sighed heavily
As if forgetting he'd been talking to me a minute ago he set off
                              in silence toward Rue Soufflot

Then I lost sight of him
I'm certain it was Merlin
For the legends lie
Merlin doesn't have the power commonly attributed to him
A maggot writhed in the remnant of the swallow's nest
                              he discarded in front of the Panthéon
With you as my witness starry night
I fear I'll never meet Merlin again

DARK CITY

I entered the dark city
Surrounded by walls
The north gate resembled the Trojan horse
The city a carousel
I walked down a street like a zeppelin
To another street with houses like windsocks
Or accordions
A bizarre building suddenly sprang up before me
An opera hat building
Beautiful women smiled at me from its windows
The next few streets comprised only beds
And suitcases
Somewhere an orchestrion was playing
A procession of blind men walked across a square the shape
                                        of a woman's hand
Cows grazed beneath a tall gallows
At the intersection a bell rang
I sat on a chair in the middle of an ebonite avenue
Where several small winged boxes hovered
Emitting a shrill song
A river chained to rails rushed toward me
It erupted into the air like a geyser right in front of me
A huge clock lay on an abandoned playground
It showed eleven p.m.
Suddenly the wind picked up
The opera hat disappeared and only large lichen remained
Huge maggots crawled from the blown-open windows

I sped toward the south gate
Where there was a park
A bush speaking human languages transfixed me most of all
And an incredible aloe with a streaming mane
A pack of dogs ran out of mirrors
And headed toward the east gate
Where there was a deep forest
I called out and no one answered
I searched for the beautiful women
I searched for the blind men
Dusk fell
I saw phosphorescent gardens
A Geissler-tube carriage pulled up to me
I got in and let it take me to the lake
A dinghy was my salvation
As soon as I'd pushed off from shore the dark city collapsed
Replaced by a great fiery inferno

Between the teeth of days a rose glistens
A sky-blue rose
Once or twice a year
Several in a lifetime
Glistens
In the window of sweet awakening
On the road of freedom
My morning thought will race down with a summer pinwheel
In a nightshirt like a butterfly
With no responsibility to settle any scores
Yesterday is forgotten
A cyclist rides past
White as Mercury
Swallow beaks peck at the surface of streams
A chimney floats like a sailboat
A hamlet glows with its opal
A hamlet wild geese fly over
What a simple ode to freedom
A bleak dream is completely erased from the blackboard
And should it stick its claws out of a muddy ditch like a scorpion
I will choose instead a spring with the shaky handwriting
                        of a water scavenger beetle
Carefree as blue vitriol dissolving
Without remorse
Breathing in lungfuls of air like clover
Under a sky clear as the shouts of a glassman
A mysterious stranger has arrived

With spyglass in hand
Wherever he points it daisies bloom
He joyfully brings the whole landscape to life
Hens are clucking
And I read a travelogue
In love like the protagonist with an island woman
A native beauty
With freshwater clamshells around her neck
And her gaze a violet tinge like the ocean
I read an exciting story about freedom
I command rebels
While bees swarm above my head
I wish they would fly away to the woods
How lovely to live inside a hollow tree
Without any queen
Without exhausting labor
For flying from blossom to blossom cannot be called
                                        by this sorry name
It's an old habit of mine
I would like to stay true to forever
On its account I'm hounded by a human hatred
That tore the rose and placed a sword between the teeth of days
I invoke a final anarchy
Encompassing a truly subtle order
Most frequently revealed by chance
Like the story about the native girl revealed to me
                                        the woman I have long loved
I see a generation coming that will act on no timetable
But according to the color of the sky
Like I write my poems

Each day brings us a different gospel
The time has now come to gain sight
For poet and mailman alike
They will first enter the house where they're most expected
And will not let my wait be long
For the telegram that humankind has definitively chosen
                                        the idea of freedom

Humankind with whom I empathize
Though not with its cowardly pangs of conscience
But everything that one day will cause it mass vertigo
Its impending unbelievable sensibilities
Resembling my poetry
And the poetry of my friends
As there is a handful of us who are more and more
                                        in complete accord

Despised as heretics
But a thousand things are still left to be said
Listen to the dictaphone of the forest
If we knew how to activate it
To the disc of night
That passed through the labyrinth of our despair
And how spectacular it will be once womanhood speaks
Once adolescence speaks once childhood speaks
In a language we decipher like cryptograms
It will be simple
Like a cabbage rose
In the balm of this morning
In whose inkpot I dip my pen
To place it between the pinwheel's fingers

TALISMAN

1.

Speaking in images
Is like pressing roses
A single rose
The rose of two lips estranged
For so long a kiss is born
Or a spell
For so long a butterfly flutters off
For so long night falls on the eyes

2.

Wait patiently
For the teardrop to wash out
From your rolled-back eye
That gigantic object
The object of your secret thoughts
You will realize
Only thanks to this mote
Is a bundle of keys
That will fit every door
Fit every extinguished lantern

3.

A teardrop falls
And reflects the whole world
Complex like a clever toy

It is a paper napkin folded by fever
Nights of love in its corners
A gold ducat in its center
That thinks for you while you sleep

4.

Look at the mark a coatrack has left
On the wall of the closet
And you will see your meager desires
A woman or city
Thus has death appeared to many

5.

Let the evening think for you
It will tell you so many of your thoughts
That you will be a thousand times wiser than the book
That tortured you
Before you thought to lift it to the garden
Or to the plow just finished plowing
That you will be a thousand times luckier than the lucky winner
Into whose lap fell all the riches of Isfahan

6.

Mold gnaws at bread crust
And builds a city
Like the emperors of Rome
And like the centuries have swept away emperors
The city is swallowed by a thrush
Whose droppings a pauper uses to plug a crack in a window

7.

A wrong can never be righted
So let us not mourn yesterday
I never expect tomorrow to be a yesterday retouched with a brush

8.

One tooth and one tooth are two teeth
Sixteen teeth and sixteen teeth are a set

9.

Such a beautiful morning
In the window behind my back
That I do not even dare
Turn my head
To avoid bursting into tears
From regret I'm no farmer
Or child
Who jumped out the window right into the river
Or onto the road
At least in this way I propel the child's hoop

10.

When foggy autumn comes
These lines will be full of summer
Oh bees
Give my reader strength
And raise a leafy tree over them
To filter autumn's poisonous wind

11.

A dead woman lay on a straw mat
They carried her into the yard
And the hens clucked
For the rosary between her fingers
Resembled dried peas
But the dead woman was not revived

12.

The woods are so far away
They resemble violins
On which a lumberjack plays pizzicato

13.

She pulled up the pail
From the well where the sky fell
And fixed her blue eyes on me
But both were just optical illusions

14.

Geraniums flower in the window
And a woman in a nightshirt
Who flits across the room
Is the moon
How I love to look into windows when it's full

15.

Morning greeting of shutters
Has startled the pigeons
For the entire village awakens to a fire breaking out
In the East
Only I sleep
And some babes in cradles
For if we woke up
The alarm would sound
Because the morning sun is red
But sleepers do not know it
Or else they would chase the red rooster into the woods

16.

I carry my talisman
Though deep in my heart
I will never lose it
As long as I stay true
To my silencing of thought
For only when the mill stops
Will you hear the lark
That will never dare screech
Will you hear the brook
Sing pianissimo
Will you hear raindrops
And lovers' words:
Devotion for devotion

CLOUDS

Your right eye is the midday sky
With a pupil of the sun at its apex
Your left eye is a pond at noon
And clouds
They are your hallucinations
When you think about love
A ship at sea
Or Africa
When you are afraid
A scorpion scurries out of the clouds
Judging by the fish you're thinking of your hands
Your longing for a wedding may be revealed by a cabbage rose
Your boredom has constructed a fantastical city
Your unease is a battle of Tritons
Are you sad that candles are being lit?
In a sealed letter you send me a quick kiss
Your joy bangs on cymbals
When you desire the whole world is behind a fence
What's on your mind that a lamp has suddenly appeared?
I see a nightshirt so you're about to go to bed?
Are you singing a lullaby because so many newborns are up there?
The down pillows betray your sleepiness
The sun now setting you sleep
And open your eyes from a dream
The right one in the sky
And the left in a lake
Your pupil is the moon

Clouded with the white of your fitful dream
You dream of your girlhood
And ravens fly from a marble castle
You dream of your first kiss
And a vulture swoops into a well
You dream of your wedding night
And a swan dies
You dream of your old age
And a ball of yarn rolls across the floor
Today you have a dreamless night
Not a single cloud in the sky
Only the morning star reveals to me your tears at dawn

Red poppy ignites barns
Or dries out
Like a scab
The guillotine felled the grass long ago
The earth resembles a wicker bread basket
Or a pincushion
The sun bleeds like a severed head
In the wicker on the horizon
Only mornings resemble crystal wells
How I would love to head out in their sky-blue beret
And not return
Except at evening
When nameless children light fires in the fields
Like Walpurgis Night
And stubble fields turn into a May brocade
Bedecking spring as it rolls into towns
Bringing hanging gardens
Towns that have been emptier than a junk shop
Turn into a game of dominoes
At midnight marionettes amble through them
A key glitters in their hand
And a candle
They go past squares that resemble an old carriage
I see fires that remind me of the town
The Pied Piper passed through
Where everyone is asleep
An owl circling above

I see fires paying homage to vineyards
The sky is overladen with grapes
And a squadron makes haste
I hear horse hooves and trumpeters
With the greatcoat of night
Bidding farewell to the accordion of summer
Whose bellows howl like forests
Some lovers having sighed
The last fire dies down like a whistle in a belfry
Good night summer
We didn't get our fill of you
Like life has flowed past us
Through a fishing net
Over the rushes where we chased will-o'-the-wisps
Like our youth has flowed past us
Under the fountain where a broken jug gleamed
Like water flows
Under the bridge over which we've spent all of eternity
Good night summer
Just one more quick kiss

LUNAR EVENING

Today the city resembles
A white rose
A violin
And a seashell
It is night and a dove coos
Let's open all the windows to the streets
And the city will in an instant be like
A powdered bosom
A white glove
And a silver wig

CELEBRATION

The last days of summer are Easter eggs
Bearing the inscription:
In honor of swallows

FAREWELL

Farewell images
That have slipped through my fingers like a potato beetle
Again I will look for dried tobacco leaves in women's eyes
Or the crackling flame
In the lamp of a funereal evening
Today the autumn crocus made me wistful
I listen to the little bells of fantastical cows
Whose swaying gait carries off the marble city

AN OMEN

A moth has landed on this manuscript of poems
Will you fly to the light or to darkness?

THE SPIRIT OF CORRUPTION

This world in which man rules over man disgusts me
And a humanity that does not want this world's day of reckoning
                                        disgusts me even more
But what disgusts me most is my own impotence to bring
                                        its murderers to reckoning
Especially since they are few enough
For me to strangle with my bare hands
I would scrub up like a doctor
Recomb my hair a bit
And go write my poetry

This world in which man rules over man disgusts me
And a humanity that does not want this world's day of reckoning
                                        disgusts me even more
But what disgusts me most is the fool who laughs at this
                                        desperate poem of mine
Which is how I should end all my books

In the summer of 1935, Vítězslav Nezval, already one of the most prolific poets of his generation, embarked on a period of profound creativity that would result in three volumes of poetry written and published in two years. These books would reshape Czech poetry, placing it at the pinnacle of the European interwar avant-garde while blending the nation's cultural sensibility and political concerns with the techniques of French Surrealism and Nezval's own unique voice. The first of these collections, *Woman in the Plural* (1936), has never before been translated into English.

As the title suggests, many of these poems focus on women, both as individuals and as archetypes. Women appear here in all shapes, sizes, and dispositions. These are the females of modern Europe, of "a single city / Through which flow the Seine Neva and Vltava." They are the fashionable urbanites of the 1930s and the timeless women of Nezval's anomalous imagination. Contemplation of the female figure is a process of fascination and creative meditation for Nezval's poetics, and the images of women are spun like a zoetrope to create a hallucinatory coalescence while displaying new ways of conceiving the female form that privilege woman's mythical, divine, creative power.

Nezval had always been a deeply romantic poet, idyllic in his evocations of amorous dusks in springtime Prague. His innate interests and sensitivities in this collection are coupled with the fiercely protean imagery of Surrealism, whose growing influence in Czech avant-garde circles led to more frequent communication between Paris and Prague and the foundation of The Surrealist Group in Czechoslovakia in 1934. Several of the poems in *Woman in the Plural*, particularly in the "Pont du Carrousel" section, are set in and inspired by Paris, a city that infatuated Nezval, while the prose in "Pages from a Diary" memorializes André Breton and Paul Éluard's 1935 visit to Prague, and the proudly declarative "Why I Am a Surrealist" ends by quoting Breton's famous last line of *Nadja* (1928). But Nezval was no mere acolyte. He adopted Surrealist techniques for his own ends, utilizing his infallible ear for linguistic rhythm and musicality, as well as his restless social life in Prague and his walks through the suburbs and the surrounding countryside. The result was a unique outgrowth of Surrealist poetry, more musical and nostalgically lyrical than its Parisian counterpart.

The title *Woman in the Plural* expresses the Surrealist insistence on the multiple and synchronous interpretation of reality. Salvador Dalí suggested as much in his description of what he termed the paranoiac-critical method, which through a "delirium of interpretation" encouraged artists and writers to explore and record the distortions of reality that occur during prolonged contemplation of an object or scene. For Dalí, this method was an "active" undermining of the world of reality, compared to what he considered the "passivity" of automatism. Both Breton and Louis Aragon lauded this use of the image as a drug to produce a Rimbaudian derangement of the senses that would allow the whole universe to be seen in a new light. Nezval would fully adopt this method for *The Absolute Gravedigger* (1937), the third and final volume of this loose trilogy, which we translated in 2016, and some of its hallucinatory power is evident even in *Woman in the Plural*. But the guiding principle of this collection is "objective chance," and its foundational text for the Surrealists, Lautréamont's *Les Chants de Maldoror* (1869), figures prominently. As Nezval later explains in *The Absolute Gravedigger*, ". . . an interest in those alluring objects that by chance insinuate themselves into our path — called surrealistic objects — involuntarily revealed to me in and of itself the method to use to concretize the poetic images of *Woman in the Plural . . .*"

If objective chance is one driving force of these poems, desire is another. This was no coincidence. The character of Nadja seems to be a fusion of desire and chance incarnate, and in *Mad Love*, Breton would note: "There — if his questioning is worth it — all the legal principles, having been routed, will bring him the strength of that *objective chance* which makes a mockery of what would have seemed probable. Everything humans might want to know is written upon this grid in phosphorescent letters, in letters of *desire*."[1] Surrealism's yoking of chance to desire encouraged Nezval to express his innate sense of romantic longing and to aestheticize, modernize, and subjectify reality through the process of looking and recording in writing his mind's spontaneous metamorphoses of feeling and interpretation. Nezval's suggestive images in *Woman in the Plural* are suffused with yearning, as his multifaceted focus on woman is inspired by sexual desire as much as a desire to transcend the boundaries of physical reality, time, and logic. Breton also highlighted how writing can sublimate desire, which finds expression in the energy that animates so many of these poems, such as "Shopwindows," which melds the poet's "desire for notebooks never to be written in" and his "desire for books I will never read" with his "desire for all women." These women are conduits through which the poet may confront, if not understand, all of reality. As Nezval rhapsodizes later in the same poem: "A woman and the sum of all the shopwindows and wonders of nature."

The juxtaposition of urban imagery and the natural world is typical for Nezval, who was born in rural Moravia and became an unapologetic champion of the modern European city. His political and social concerns, like many intellectuals in the 1930s, spanned from

1. André Breton, *Mad Love*, trans. Mary Ann Caws (Lincoln: University of Nebraska Press, 1987), 87.

Paris to Prague to Leningrad. Readers of *Woman in the Plural* wander European alleys and boulevards in spring and summer alongside him, a flâneur with a surfeit of imagination and time, a poet with the avant-garde wherewithal to combine his verse with metatextual diary entries recording precise moments of inspiration and composition, and detailing meetings with cultural insurgents, including the great Czech artist Toyen and the Prague-based director Jindřich Honzl, as well as those impeccable Merlins of Surrealism, Breton and Éluard.

But Nezval was also a magnificent poet of nature, and many of the poems in *Woman in the Plural* are enriched by the vastness and detail of his descriptions and depictions of Earth's minutiae. Women's hats aren't simply bedecked with flowers, but papilionaceous flowers. Fields are full of red poppies, turkeys, and carrion beetles; forests are overgrown with wide burdock leaves; rivers wind through mirabelle plums. It is a Surrealism brought out of the cafés and into the countryside by Nezval's complex poetics.

Some contemporary readers will take issue with the way that Nezval objectifies women. Many critics and theorists have grappled with the unapologetically, and at times distressingly, insistent male gaze of Surrealism, noting that its visual art and literature tend to present women as a fractured body (a common feature of Karel Teige's collages, for example). The Surrealist gaze, however, is more than mere objectification.[2] Certainly Nezval's varied descriptions of the female form are at times guilty of this fragmentation as well, but they are in large part expressions of his romantic exuberance, a lyrical excitement and innocence. *Woman in the Plural* was composed in Prague during the spring and summer of 1935, at the height of the city's modernity and fame as a European capital of culture. These poems

2. Cf. Mary Ann Caws, *The Surrealist Look: An Erotics of Encounter* (Cambridge: MIT Press, 1999).

seamlessly combine Nezval's imaginative musings with accounts of actual women he encountered on the streets of the Golden City at that most beautiful time of year. It is a poetry of praise, though darker moments of uncertainty intrude, and the women are indeed loved — even as murder victims in "The Bird of Doom."

Woman in the Plural is also indexed to the social and political instability of the 1930s, which aligns it with that decade's international modernism. Several poems in this collection reference the debacles of the early 20th century. In "Phantoms," Nezval writes of "a century of calamity and poetry," a sentiment that is echoed in "The Spirit of Corruption," which expresses disgust at a "world in which man rules over man" and the poet's own "impotence to bring its murderers to reckoning." These issues would culminate in the bleaker poems of *The Absolute Gravedigger* some 18 months later. Yet Nezval counters pre-war pessimism with the conviction that poets are here to praise and express the quotidian and marvelous beauty of the human imagination and of the world. In so doing, they might just save it.

It was not Nezval's intent to make *Woman in the Plural* an overtly political book, but as a committed communist his eye was clearly drawn to the proletariat, to glassworkers and working-class women from the city's outlying industrial districts. His humane distress about the state of society and his disenfranchisement as a poet is on display in "The Fight for the Seeing Man," which despairs over the contemporary human existence of "endless angst" where "despicable speculation" by those in power tears the bread from the lips of workers. Poetry offers hope, but it is difficult to imagine how poets, those "most human" of individuals, could "possibly have a place in this society" where they are considered lunatics. The poem is a lament for workers as fodder for capitalism and poets as outcasts from the officially established hierarchy of cultural and political values.

Nezval felt comfortable at the intersection of poetry and politics, and was likely familiar with Tristan Tzara's "Essay on the Situation of Poetry" from 1931, which argued: "a new state could be born in a communist society in which every relation of value is new, a *poetic state* dominated by non-directed thought superimposed on the structure of civilization and its indestructible conquests [...] Poetic activity alone is capable of giving a *human* conclusion to *liberation*. Dream, laziness and leisure should be organized with a view to communist society; this is poetry's most current task."[3] The magic of *Woman in the Plural* is that Nezval takes on this task by way of expressing his peculiar, confounding, compelling imagination in poems, prose, and drama of striking originality.

Nezval's masterful, profoundly playful, wildly specific writing complicates the French-centric reading of Surrealism. More than a Prague poet, or even a Czech poet, he is a major figure of the European interwar avant-garde. Even so, Nezval and his work are intimately connected to Prague, that hothouse for creative ideas from East and West alike. To live in this city is to be enveloped in the cosmopolitan urbanity of Central Europe amid the histories and cultures of surrounding nations with whom Bohemia has interacted for over a millennium. A perpetual personal expression and a document of its moment, *Woman in the Plural* presents Nezval at his most ebullient, in the summer of 1935 when World War II was only beginning to rumble over the distant hills where rain was "buckshot," geese "boisterous howitzers," and winter snow "merciless as a candle snuffer."

S.D. & T.N., PRAGUE, 2021

3. Tristan Tzara, "Essay on the Situation of Poetry," trans. Krzysztof Fijalkowski and Michael Richardson, in *The Surrealism Reader: An Anthology of Ideas* (London: Tate Publishing, 2015), 270-280.

17   *I walked past the Luxembourg Gardens:* In his memoir on his visits to
      Paris, *Rue Gît-Le-Coeur* (1936), Nezval recounts sitting a few years ear-
      lier on a June night with Benjamin Péret on the patio of Café du Dôme
      in Montparnasse. Leaving near midnight, he made his way down a
      deserted Boulevard du Montparnasse toward the Luxembourg Gardens
      where he saw the tree fruit covered in a white gauze, about which he
      remarked: "Visible through the iron fence, they truly were white blots."
      To commemorate the event he wrote "A Chemise," and included it both
      here and in *Rue Gît-Le-Coeur.*

22   *guelder rose:* In Slavic folklore, the guelder rose and its red berries are
      a symbol of the tenderness, passion, and love of young women.

42   *a ballgown in a hazelnut:* In the Czech version of "Cinderella" ("Tři
      oříšky pro Popelku"), Cinderella has three magic hazelnuts that she
      throws on the ground to make a wish. When she wishes for a gown to
      wear to the royal ball, she pulls the dress out of the hazelnut.

56   *Bulletin international du surréalisme:* A bilingual French-Czech edition
      (with the Czech title *Mezinárodní bulletin surrealismu*) published by
      the Surrealist Group in Czechoslovakia in April 1935 soon after André
      Breton and Paul Éluard's visit to Prague earlier that month, when the
      idea for an international bulletin of Surrealism was hatched.

58   *Apollinaire's "passant de Prague":* Guillaume Apollinaire's well-known
      story "Le passant de Prague," published in 1910 in the collection
      L'hérésiarque et Cie, has come into English with the unfortunate title
      "The Wandering Jew" [cf. *The Heresiarch & Co.* (Cambridge: Exact
      Change, 1991)]. While *passant* literally means "passerby," the story
      inspired Nezval's poem "Pražský chodec," which appears in *Prague with
      Fingers of Rain* as "Walker in Prague" (trans. Ewald Osers), and his
      book of memoir-like prose with the same title, *Pražský chodec* (1938)
      [forthcoming in English translation in 2021 as *A Prague Flâneur*].

63   *my pen and I:* The Czech "*já a moje péro*" here could alternately be read as "my dick and I."

107 *I'm a woman like any other:* Though this phrase is repeated throughout the play by different women, it was omitted here in the first edition from 1936. The annotated edition from 2012 (Brno: Host) includes it and points out that this decision is based on Nezval's handwritten emendation to the typescript.

115 *slowly sits up in the coffin:* Omitted in the original edition, which has only, "and the DECEASED WIFE waves her hand." It was added in the 2012 edition per Nezval's emendation to the manuscript.

115 *Forgive me. I'm a woman like any other:* Omitted in the original edition and included in the 2012 edition per Nezval's handwritten emendation to the typescript, and consistency with the rest.

137 *The tree frog:* In Central European folk tradition it was believed that tree frogs could predict the weather. When placed in a glass jar with a small ladder, the frog would climb it if forecasting clear skies or descend it if forecasting rain.

144 *For the beauty that "will be convulsive or will not be at all":* The quote comes from: André Breton, *Nadja*, trans. Richard Howard (New York: Grove Press, 1960).

147 *If you call into the woods:* Likely an allusion to the Czech proverb *Jak se do lesa volá, tak se z lesa ozývá*, meaning, "You reap what you sow," but literally: "The forest echoes back what you call into it."

168 *Knights of the Cross:* Full name: Knights of the Cross with the Red Star, an order of knights founded in 1233 by St. Agnes of Bohemia, sister of King Wenceslas I, as a hospice brotherhood. The order's monastery, Church of St. Francis, and Hospital of the Holy Spirit were built in 1252 and are located by Prague's Old Town Bridge Tower of Charles Bridge (Judith Bridge at the time of their construction).

VÍTĚZSLAV NEZVAL (1900–58) was the leading Czech avant-garde writer of perhaps the entire 20th century. A founding member of both Devětsil in 1920 and the Surrealist Group in Czechoslovakia in 1934 (the first such group outside of France), Nezval's oeuvre consists of numerous poetry collections, experimental plays and novels, memoirs, essays, and translations. In addition to *The Absolute Gravedigger*, his most important work includes *Pantomime, Prague with Fingers of Rain, Valerie and Her Week of Wonders*, and *A Prague Flâneur*. Along with Karel Teige, Jindřich Štyrský, and Toyen, Nezval frequently visited Paris and forged ties with the French Surrealists. He served as editor of the Czech group's journal *Surrealismus*.

STEPHAN DELBOS is the Poet Laureate of Plymouth, Massachusetts, and a Senior Lecturer at Charles University and Anglo-American University in Prague. A founding editor of the webzine *B O D Y*, his poetry, essays, and translations have been published internationally. His translations from Czech include *The Absolute Gravedigger* by Vítězslav Nezval and *Paris Notebook* by Tereza Riedlbauchová. He is the author of the poetry collections *Light Reading* and *Small Talk*.

TEREZA VEVERKA NOVICKÁ is a Czech California-born literary translator whose translations of Czech and Slovak poets into English, such as Ondřej Buddeus, Sylva Fischerová, Nóra Ružičková, Olga Pek, and Jan Škrob, have appeared in a number of periodicals. Her full-length translations include *The Absolute Gravedigger* by Vítězslav Nezval, *Aviaries* by Zuzana Brabcová, and the monograph *Ludvík Šváb: Tidy Up After I Die*.

KAREL TEIGE (1900–51) was the leading Czech avant-garde critic, whose many theoretical writings ranged from Dada to architecture to typography to art monographs, in addition to being a prolific collagist and book designer. A member of Devětsil, he authored its Poetist Manifesto and served as editor and graphic designer for the group's monthly journal *ReD* (Revue Devětsilu). He was a founding member of the Surrealist Group in Czechoslovakia and became its de facto head after WWII.

WOMAN IN THE PLURAL

by Vítězslav Nezval

Translated by Stephan Delbos and Tereza Novická
from the original Czech *Žena v množném čísle*
first published in 1936 by Fr. Borový in Prague

Cover image and collages by Karel Teige
from original Czech edition of 1936

Design by Silk Mountain

Set in Garamond Pro / Univers

FIRST EDITION OF 1000 COPIES IN HARDCOVER

Published in 2021

Twisted Spoon Press
P.O. Box 21 – Preslova 12
150 00 Prague 5
Czech Republic
www.twistedspoon.com

Printed and bound in the Czech Republic by Akcent

Trade distribution

UK & Europe
CENTRAL BOOKS
www.centralbooks.com

US & Canada
SCB DISTRIBUTORS
www.scbdistributors.com